Wisdom for a Young Musician

Wisdom

for a

Young Musician

by Bruce Warren

RUNNING PRESS
PHILADELPHIA • LONDON

World Cafe® is a registered trademark of the Trustees of the
University of Pennsylvania.
This book may not be reproduced in whole or in part, in any form or by
any means, electronic or mechanical, including photocopying, recording, or
by any information storage and retrieval system now known or
hereafter invented, without written permission from the publisher.

9   8   7   6   5   4   3   2   1
Digit on the right indicates the number of this printing

Library of Congress Control Number: 2006938868

ISBN-10: 0-7624-2861-9
ISBN-13: 978-0-7624-2861-8

Cover and interior designed by Alicia Freile
Edited by Greg Jones
Typography: Alexa, Minion, and Univers

This book may be ordered by mail from the publisher.
Please include $2.50 for postage and handling.
But try your bookstore first!

Running Press Book Publishers
2300 Chestnut Street
Philadelphia, Pennsylvania 19103-4371

A member of the Perseus Books Group

Visit us on the web!
www.runningpress.com

For musicians everywhere.

"Music is its own reward . . . it will nourish your soul whether or not you become a platinum-selling artist."

—Sting

CONTENTS

INTRODUCTION

Write songs.

Play out a lot—perform in public as much as you can.

Completely own the songs you write.

Offer free songs on your Web site.

Start a blog to connect with your fans.

Take advantage of the new platforms available to you
    to reach music fans.

Podcast your music.

YouTube it.

Don't expect much, if any, radio play.

This book contains incredible advice for young musicians from some of the best-known and lesser-known artists today, alongside words of wisdom from folks in the music industry who have managed artists or promoted records or tour-managed musicians.

A week hasn't passed during my career when I haven't received a call or an e-mail from a musician just starting out who wants to know how to get their record played on the radio, or what they need to do to kick-start their career.

I usually start to verbalize the list above. But then I start to dig a little deeper.

To the first question, I answer something like: "Write a song as good as Radiohead or U2 or Jackson Browne or Neil Young or Sting or Joni Mitchell or (enter your favorite artist here)." But we all know that you can write the pop masterpiece of all time and the chances will still be slim that it will get on the radio at all. Some of the best songs in any genre of music that should have been hits have come and gone. And that will continue. The truth is, as a musician you need to find a sustainable strategy for making music your full-time career and, while I wish you all the luck writing and then having a chart-topping hit song, my suggestion is to think more broadly and to focus on the various ways you can get your music out to the people. I tell musicians that they need to do everything they can to "find their voice."

Ultimately it starts with you and your guitar or piano, in your bedroom or your living room on your Mac or PC or four-channel mixing board. The beauty of our multi-platform world is that with very affordable new technology and a DSL line you can be a recording musician very easily. And you can promote your music and let people hear it without breaking the bank.

Many of the quotes and notes you will read in this book are from visiting musicians to *World Cafe®*, a two-hour daily radio program hosted and produced by David Dye and distributed to over 180 stations across North America by NPR (National Public Radio). Each day on the *Cafe*, a band does an interview and performance, talks to Dye about their craft, and tells him their stories. Every musician has plenty of stories! And here you will read pearls of wisdom that hopefully will inspire your work or improve your mindset as you grow into this incredible career you've chosen as a musician.

We could not have created this book without the help from the following folks. Special thanks to the programming staff at WXPN-FM in Philadelphia: Tracey Tanenbaum, who produced "A Musician's Life" series and who did the interviews with these artists; Nikki Avershaw, who listened to hundreds of hours of *World Cafe* interviews; Roger LaMay, General Manager of WXPN; David Dye of *World Cafe;* Quyen Shanahan and Kim Winnick. Thanks to The MusicLab© at *World Cafe Live* for access to the interviews. Also thanks to Greg Jones and Alicia Freile of Running Press; Gary Kaplan, Danny Hest, and Vivek Tiwary of Starpolish.com; and to all the musicians who contributed their words of wisdom.

The advice shared in this book is invaluable no matter where you are in your career. Even if you're not in the music business but are interested in music, this book will be a revelation. But for all the musicians out there, we hope it inspires you to reach your wildest dreams. And as Neil Young once said, "Long may you run."

1

STARTING OUT

"You have to find your unique voice as a musician and be prepared to be committed, because this can take years."

—Charlotte Martin
Songwriter, singer, and keyboardist

The most important thing to remember is that starting out all starts with you—your art, your voice, your personality, your convictions, and your passions. You will hear over and over from the musicians and others in this book about the "music business," and you will see how the "music" and the "business" will stand both alone and together as you pursue your art and your career.

Ultimately, the journey begins with questions only you can answer. And no matter how far you take your career, it always comes back to questions like: Who am I? What do I sound like? What do I look like? What kind of impact do I want to have? How do I want my fans to perceive me and my music? All of these questions are justifiable and important to ask. Remember this: We all have strengths and weaknesses. We all have goals we want to achieve. And as you plan your road map, never compromise who you are and what you want, yet always be open to feedback from the people you trust the most.

You will read a lot of excellent advice here: Get a good lawyer. Follow your instincts. Play out as much as you can. Start a great Web site. Give your music away for free. Don't give your music away for free. Surround yourself with trustful people. Get involved with the business side. Let someone else handle your business affairs. Just go for it. Get enough sleep and eat healthy. Practice a lot. Practice more than a lot. Challenge yourself to always do better. And ultimately, love what you do.

Marc A. Roberge

Rhythm guitarist and lead singer of O.A.R.

In my experience I find that there is one simple rule to this business of music. More specifically, being an artist in the music business. You must absolutely, at your core, love what you are doing. It sounds cliché and probably the last bit of advice someone looking for guidance wants to hear. I find, however, that what will ultimately shape your journey through a career in music is your level of belief. At the beginning stages when you face crowds more interested in hearing "Freebird" than your newest ballad, you better love what you do. When shady bar owners try and convince you that your personal tab somehow made the night a wash, you better love what you do. And when you get the always-pleasant question from Mom asking if you will ever get a "real" job, you better love what you are doing.

After you have played every open mic in town and are finally developing your sound, off to the studio you go. You print up 1,000 discs via Disc Makers, have your buddy create some fantastic artwork, and put them out for the world to see at your next gig. You sell five. To your mom. Who is still asking if you are sure this is a "real" job. You better love what you do. And finally when you have gotten that record "deal" and everyone loves you, your debut record comes out, sells 5,000 copies, and everyone suddenly disappears. You had better, absolutely, at your core, love what you do. It's simple. The music business is a hard, stressful beast to tame. Music, however, is a universally beautiful language. If you love what you do, playing in local bars will be a treat, writing songs will be a gift, and telling Mom that being a musician is in fact a real job will be one of the most liberating days of your life.

"When we first started we decided we'll do this whenever we can until we get to a point where we can do it full time."

—Warren Haynes, Government Mule

"Just be yourself. Even when you try to copy someone, your own personality is still gonna come through. So why not just quit trying to do that and just be yourself."

—Oteil Burbridge

"How did I start? I just started out playing cover songs in bars in Ottawa. You have to start somewhere with something."

—Kathleen Edwards

"All of the technical ability in the world really doesn't mean anything if you can't make that transition to playing music."

—Sonny Landreth

Carbon Leaf

For the Musician:

1. Practice a lot on your own and with your band. I have also found that playing along to the radio (even to songs you don't like) is also a good way to learn new stuff.

2. Take lessons. Find a good teacher that can teach you about music theory in general as well as your specific instrument.

3. Use your ears and follow your instinct. You know what you like, so don't be afraid to follow a different creative path if that is what a song needs. Conversely, if you have a feeling that something isn't working or that it sounds bad, then you are probably right and should approach things differently.

4. Learn some piano. The piano is a great foundation for all types of music, so it will help you with your music theory and in arranging songs for a band. Also, you can use a piano-style key-

board controller (we use an M-audio Oxygen 8) plugged into a computer to control all kinds of software—giving you access to sounds as diverse as strings, drums, bagpipes, and weird synths.

5. Learn a little (maybe a lot!) about computers and try recording your band's rehearsals into a program like Cakewalk, Pro Tools, Logic, GarageBand, etc. This will allow you to a) hear what your songs actually sound like, b) make demos to get gigs, and c) make MP3s to put on the web.

For the Band:
1. Get a good lawyer and don't sign anything without running it by them first. You don't need a big-shot entertainment lawyer at this stage, just a trusted friend of the family who will give you honest (and cheap!) advice.

2. Start a Web site and put up free downloads of your songs.

3. Start an e-mail newsletter.

4. Buy the best gear that you can get, but . . .

5. . . . beware of credit cards.

6. Ford E-350 Vans (with either the V10 or diesel engine) are great for touring.

FOCUS ON ART

"When you're interviewed, never talk about marketing details because it's a huge turn-off. It makes you sound like an advertising executive, not an artist. Listeners want to think of you as such and are willing to grant you certain powers as long as your credibility remains intact. Talking about release dates, advertising plans and other minutiae of the music business diminishes your credibility and your power. That said—make sure you pay attention! Do not abdicate business responsibilities to managers/lawyers/record companies/etc. These people are there to support you, but the sooner you realize that no one will ever care about your career as much as you, the better. And, if you're lucky enough to be successful and you haven't paid attention to the business side, you're gonna get screwed. As Little Richard advises: 'sign the checks!'"

—Sean Coakley
Founder and president, Songlines LTD (music marketing and promotion)

The Groundrules

(Excerpted from "The Groundrules," from Starpolish.com.)

1. Study your instruments from a traditional perspective first.

Even if your sound and songs defy structure and revolve around atypical sonic elements, know how to play cleanly and write simply first. We believe that to thwart a system, you need to know that system—that goes for the art as well as the business. You can't make good abstract art unless you know from what you are abstracting. If you hate the current state of music and you want to turn modern songwriting and performance on its head, know what the head looks like when it's right-side up. If you consider the greatest abstract/surrealist artists of all time and study their early work, you will see that they mastered the traditional elements of their art before pushing the envelope.

2. Consider lessons for technique, not just sound.

Art is to some extent a learned process—even prodigies can benefit from lessons. You may be a pro at playing your instrument or singing, but lessons can invaluably help with your technique, and they will provide saving tips—so that when you go on a major tour and play five days in a row, you still have a voice, your drummer's hands aren't about to snap at the wrist, etc. Lessons can be expensive, but they're worth looking into. At the least, books, though they can't replace a real-life teacher, are better than nothing.

3. Study your favorite songs.

There are many songwriting workshops and lessons that might be helpful in honing your craft, but we suggest that you first sit in front of your stereo with a pad and pencil, put on your favorite songs, and take notes. Ask yourself what is it about those songs that you like so much. It's also useful to study songs that have been recent hits (even if you don't want to write a popular hit, this exercise is interesting). Which of these hits do you like and which do you hate? Why? Are there any traits they all share? When doing these exercises, think not just about song structure and sonic elements, but about lyrics and content. Bruce Springsteen once said that he learned more from three-minute records than he ever did in school. And while we don't advocate not going to school or taking lessons, songwriters could indeed benefit from The Boss's advice.

4. Get feedback on your practices.

Occasionally, invite some friends whose opinions you trust to your practices and solicit their feedback. Remember that advice is often most helpful during the work-in-progress phase, and not when material is complete.

5. Video and audiotape everything.

Audiotape your practices and shows for later review. You'll often hear things on tape—both good and bad—that you didn't notice during the performance. Videotape as much as possible. You might be surprised to see how you look during a performance, and these videotapes might suggest ways to improve your image and stage presence. These video and audiotapes need not be of high quality—they are for your eyes and ears only. When you become a famous success, these audio and videotapes will be a valuable part of your archives. We know you may not be thinking that far ahead, but that brings us to our last point. . . .

6. Always think about the future.

In order to be successful in this business, spend a *small* part of your time and efforts thinking about the long, long term. The best time to plan for the future is in the past.

JUST GO FOR IT

"Because there were just two of us, we just wanted to flesh out the sound as much as possible, and we had enough difference in our own voices to make it interesting. So we just went for it very early on, with staggered harmonies and trying to pick interesting notes, not just going for the one, three, five. Trying to keep it as interesting and expansive as possible was at our core from the very beginning."

—Emily Saliers
Indigo Girls

PLAY, PLAY, PLAY

"When I was first writing and performing, I asked my friend and producer, Phil Nicolo (Grammy-winning producer for Bob Dylan, John Lennon, Sting, and Lauryn Hill) the question: 'What should I be doing now to establish and further my career?' I thought he might say, 'Start calling record labels, find a manager, make a record,' etc. Instead, he replied with the most important thing I've learned to date with regard to music: 'Play, play, play, put your head down and keep on playing! Play every night, if you can!' I think he even added, 'Play open mics, bars, cafés, streets, subways, 7-11 parking lots!'

Phil may have been speaking in hyperbole, but the point was well taken. I interpreted this to mean that the way to become great at what you do, is to DO IT!

Phil's advice was very sound—no pun intended."

—John Francis
Singer-songwriter

Brian Seymour

"Don't look sideways."

I was young and ambitious, but there I was, in over my head, five minutes from running panicked out of a meet-and-greet party in a swanky club in NYC. As luck would have it, a rather well-established and well-oiled NYC songwriter with more than a few hits in his pocket barreled into me, cheap white wine and all. After just a few minutes of chatting, he kindly raised his hand (possibly as a way to break the flurry of questions I was nervously spouting) and he said something I will never forget: "Don't look sideways."

What I took from that little exchange became a guiding principle in my creative life—we certainly all need mentors and paths to follow, but shouldn't get wrapped up in worrying what the other guy is doing. Too many young artists spin their wheels fretting over everyone else's killer contacts and great press. This quickly leads to burnout, and artists can lose sight of why they began creating music in the first place.

Another jewel came from songwriter/producer Richard Gottehrer at an ASCAP (American Society of Composers, Authors and Publishers) workshop. He said simply, "Just keep writing songs." These are words I live by. If you don't believe that your best work is still ahead, you're done. We should all be wary of music-biz sharks who offer shortcuts to yesterday's hit sound; what catches is a song that is unique and breaks the form, not one that repeats it.

"Sleep is one of the most important things for singers, because the voice really responds to that."

—Michael McDonald

"Develop the skills to execute what you feel."

—Joe Sample

IT'S NOT ABOUT THE BENJAMINS

"Do not become a musician if you want to make money right away. Handling a career is just like handling a small business: there are risks and rewards and, more likely than not, you'll spend more than you make in the beginning. You'll need a support system financially whether it's someone who believes in your music and wants to help, no strings attached, or someone who is willing to invest and wait to get their money back. Make sure you have someone to lean on."

—**Melody Gardot**
Blues, folk, and jazz-influenced singer-songwriter

Charlotte Martin

Songwriter, singer, and keyboardist

Q&A

1. What kinds of advice were you given when you were first starting out and who gave it to you?

When I first started out writing and recording, I was a senior in college about to graduate. My plan after graduation was to a) Go to graduate school in voice (I wanted to be a professor) or b) Move to LA or NY and try to make it as an artist/composer. My dad actually advised me to move to LA and go for a career as an artist. I was serious about becoming a composer and he thought I had more of a shot doing it as a recording artist.

I was fortunate enough to be able to write with Carole King very early on in my writing stages of "On Your Shore." We wrote two songs together and during that process she asked me of my lyric choices in our song, "What Is the Point?" After the Carole sessions, I went through a period of writing less abstractly which shined a new light on my lyrics. I needed to learn all ways to write to eventually develop my own style which has basically taken 10 years. *She is an amazing songwriter, and she*

can write lyrics to the point, or paint a Monet or both and more.
She is a true genius.

2. What would you say are the three or four most important things a young musician should focus on when they are just starting out?

First, you have to find your unique voice as a musician and be prepared to be committed because this can take years. But it's all about the process, in my opinion. Second, I would build your live show through rehearsal, rehearsal, rehearsal, trial and error on your set, production, hiring musicians, or gear. Third, I would research and invest in some small recording situation whether it be on a laptop or with an Mbox. Make your own music, duplicate it . . . use it to book shows and start selling it on the Internet. Make your music accessible in as many ways as you possibly can. If your music is good, the listeners and people to help you will find you. What's meant to be will be, if you prepare to put yourself in a position for your path.

3. What's the most difficult part of the business of music and what do you suggest that musicians should learn about in maintaining control of their careers?

I would say the most difficult thing for me in the business side of my career was surrounding myself with people I could trust with my life, art, money, deals, marketing, fans.

An artist that lives on the road and is in the business of touring and actively releasing records on any level, will at least have 10 or 12 people working with them or their personal manager. I went through a period in my early career when I was too immature to want to know what was going on which I regret in some respects. I just wasn't ready to handle both the business and the art. Needless to say, I learned through trial and error that I will always need to know what's going on in my career on some level. I have been around the block long enough to know that I have to work with people I trust and to end working relationships where that trust has been compromised. Not everyone in the world is out to help you, you know. As an artist who is in the business of art, you have to protect it from the people who could do wrong things and not have your art's best intentions, if you know what I mean.

4. What advice would you give musicians to learn to cope with both positive and negative feedback they get from fans and music critics?

I am very picky with reviews. I would rather read interviews. I only like to read negative reviews if my manager or publicist think they are relevant to making me a better artist, performer, producer, etc. The reviews that trash for no reason other than the critic doesn't like it and think you suck, there's nothing you can get out of that but bad energy. So I have them screened. There are a lot of critical comments sent to my team and they listen, and I listen when there is something said. Both the positive and negative can be teachers and help in the growth of the music.

5. What advice do you have for being on the road and balancing the need for personal time and creative time?

I have a strict schedule when I'm touring. I don't write on the road. . . . I can't write Charlotte Martin records when I'm touring because I'm focusing all that I am as an artist on the shows and the fans. I don't know what personal time is. Just kidding. I take an hour every morning whether I'm at home recording or doing press . . . or touring. I pray and read and meditate. I have to be in touch with my spirit and the One that gives me my strength. It's my way of filling myself up so I can give myself away to the music, fans, or creative process.

6. What are the unexpected consequences of being a musician and what would you tell a young artist to be on the lookout for or be aware of?

On a business side, remember to budget. Remember to be wise with your money and not spend it all as soon as you make it because you will run into periods where you have a significant time when things are tight and the work isn't flowing in as much. Just stay as balanced in this area as possible and you'll be okay. I'm not saying to be a miser either because you have to invest in your career to do anything. Just be balanced about it.

7. What personal qualities do you need to be a musician?

Inspiration, passion, discipline, insanity, insomnia, pitch memory is always nice, and being committed, loyal, fierce and humble.

8. What are three things you like best about being a musician?

My fans, touring, and producing.

9. Being in the studio by yourself and being on stage in front of people are two different things. What advice would you give to a musician first playing out in public?

You can never play too many shows. That is my opinion because I think every show makes you better and better on all levels. Play everywhere you can and anytime you can . . . and your artistry will grow so fast you won't even notice it until you take time off and play another show. It will be interpreted on a new level and you'll learn new things from your own music.

10. If you have ever had a "writer's block" what kind of things did you do to get out of it?

I don't believe in writer's block. But I believe there are times when I'm writing complete shit. I would call this "uninspired writing" instead of writer's block. I can write myself empty and then I have to stop. I'm totally terrified of this period but I use it to fill up again. Impassionate writing is like eating when you're not hungry. No point.

11. What do you draw inspiration from?

I draw inspiration from life—my personal experiences with people . . . which are enough right there. Also film, books, other music inspires me.

12. How do you cope—and what advice would you give a young musician in coping—with a setback in your career?

When I first got signed, my record I worked on for a year was shelved. It took several months to knock myself out of a severe depression. It's like watching something slowly die. I mourned over it too long. It was the writing process of my next record that eventually brought me out of the pit. You have to get up at some point and keep going. The music called me . . . it just took time. I felt like a lover that got dumped. It was too painful to make music for a while because I was so afraid it would be squashed on, but eventually my drive to create outweighed my depression and morphed into my therapy for not only the record being shelved, but all negative trials that are thrown at me.

"It's very important to be meticulous in practice."

—Sonny Landreth

"I think for any young person starting off who plays an instrument, live with that instrument as much as you can and learn that instrument as well as you can."

—Michael McDonald

> ## "Every arranger in town hired me . . . once."
>
> —Warren Zevon

> "Someone once said to me, 'When you sign a record deal, two things happen: you hate the record company and your friends hate you.' People get very weird when success comes your way. Don't get bigheaded but don't go out of your way to appease everyone. You deserve it. Now work your ass off to keep it."
>
> —Scot Sax

Ingrid Michaelson

Singer-songwriter and pianist

Q&A

1. What would you say are the three or four most important things a young musician should focus on when they are just starting out?

Getting a great demo/CD. You want a great product to give/sell that accurately represents your current sound.

Get a Web site.

Try to play consistently, but not only in one town.

Be persistent in your endeavors, but never pushy . . . you have to toe the line!

2. What advice would you give musicians to learn to cope with both positive and negative feedback they get from fans and music critics?

You have got to be confident in your abilities, bottom line. If you do, criticism will be interesting and informative, not painful. You should listen to every bit of feedback, not only the good. I find the negative criticism pushes me to try new things.

3. What are three things you like best about being a musician?

Writing and singing gives me an outlet for my emotions.

Your music can affect a perfect stranger.

I am leaving pieces of myself wherever I sing; I think that's pretty cool.

4. If you have ever had a "writer's block" what kind of things did you do to get out of it?

I don't force myself. I'll take a break for a couple weeks and not try to write anything. I also listen to new music to get newness in my head—new themes, new structures.

"I always played with musicians who were older than me, and it really was rough on me, because I really wasn't good enough to play with them. But you know when people are higher than you, it just pulls you up."

—Oteil Burbridge

"No matter what kind of music you're gonna make, you oughta understand and have some kind of appreciation for all kinds of music."

—Big Kenny & John Rich (Big & Rich)

"I didn't really start playing until I was 19 or 20 years old and I started writing right away. I got a guitar, learned a couple of chords, and started writing tunes."

—Amos Lee

"I'm at the mercy of other songwriters and journalists and radio people as I travel around. On tour I'm always asking people who they know and who they've heard from under the radar, and I have boxes of CDs sent to me from all over—you never know when you're going to find the next Tom Waits or Neil Young."

—Bonnie Raitt

Jack Barton

Senior Director, *Friday Morning Quarterback*

It seems one of the hardest things for a fledgling artist to understand is the balance between work and fun, as well as art and commerce. Understand that once you choose to make a living at your art, you are now in the *business* of art. Look for and accept constructive criticism and advice—both creatively and marketing/business-wise. Understand that if you're gonna quit your day job, business concerns are as important as the creative ones. But don't lose the essence of your art. A tricky endeavor, indeed.

Challenge yourself, on a daily basis, to be better. Better at songwriting, performing, recording—everything you do. Accept and be proud of what you do well, but focus on what you can do better. Even when you're exceeding your initial expectations, reflect on what's gone both wrong and right, and figure out how you can improve it. You'll never write the perfect song, you'll never do the perfect show, and you'll never make the perfect record. But you'll be a hell of a lot more satisfied and have a boatload more fun—and probably have greater success—if you never allow complacency to settle in.

Learn the business. There are plenty of books in the library that explain publishing, touring, record deals, and most everything else you need to know. Your intellectual property (i.e. your songs) and your live performances are your greatest assets. Even if you have management, understanding your rights and the machinations of the industry means you don't need to blindly trust anyone else to look out for your well-being.

Finally, WORK. Play every show you can get. Especially when you're starting out. Open mics, gigs you lose money on; it doesn't matter. Get out of your hometown. The more people that have a chance to hear you in more places, the quicker you'll build your own fan base and be able to work on your own terms. And good luck.

"None of us thought we would be making a living out of it. . . ."

—Guster

"It seemed like whatever we did was always being revised."

—They Might Be Giants

> **"My favorite music isn't always played in tune or in time."**
>
> —Sonny Landreth

> *"To really understand the instrument, you have to play it."*
>
> —Joe Bonamassa

Jeff Cook

Head of Promotion, New West Records

Having been a working musician, written songs for bands, worked in record stores, and now having spent the last 25 years working for record companies, doing radio promotion on the local, regional and national levels, I have had the opportunity to watch and work with some of the most successful artists in the business. This has resulted in quite an education with regard to the cultivation of a career in music.

However, I must begin with my usual disclaimer . . . that my opinion of MY opinion has gone down every year I have been in the business! When I was 20, there wasn't anything I didn't know . . . and there certainly wasn't much you could tell me either! Experience has shown me clearly, that if you think you know best, you don't! There is always more to learn and there are ALWAYS exceptions to the rules! (That, of course, gives you a lot of latitude.)

The most common thing I see with musicians that are just starting off, is that they ALWAYS think they should be further along than they are, that if only they could get the right gigs, the right manager, the right label deal, all their problems would be solved. I disagree, all of these things help but a career is a process and all things come in time. Each of these things has to be earned and every successful artist I have worked with has had to do a lot of work to get there. Not just playing the gigs but learning the business, the politics of dealing with others and growing into success.

I am a believer in the "build it and they will come theory." Everything starts with you and ends with YOU! How much will you do in the name of your OWN growth? Meaning, if you want the right high profile show . . . are you willing to play tiny clubs, house parties or anywhere that will get the buzz going? If you want the right manager, are you willing to build your own profile to the point that a real experienced manager with a track record will hear about you? Are you willing to invest in your own recordings (it's never been cheaper with today's technology), sell them at gigs to friends/fans; and use them to help promote you at radio/retail/press?

In the broadest of strokes, be COMMITTED to yourself and others will be drawn, be FLEXIBLE so others can work with you. (You don't need to sign away your publishing, but maybe you do a deal on a song-by-song basis, to get the ball rolling.) Be WILLING to do whatever it takes to keep moving forward. Be FOREWARNED this is one of the most competitive businesses out there and you must be prepared to step up and do what needs to be done.

The good news is that if you LOVE what you do, the sacrifices seem more like opportunities. The hard work seems like a joy and the success you may or may not find, will just be icing on the cake!

Confucius said in 563 B.C., "Do what you love and you will never work a day in your life!" For me that has rung true for over 30 years.

WATCH OUT!

"At the age of 21, I signed my first record deal and became a Warner Brothers recording artist. Over the past 25 years I've had enough record deals, production deals, and publishing deals to fill a chapter of this book. Realize this: The music business is a minefield filled with lies, deceit, and uncertainty. You have to be skilled, lucky, or a combination of both. Your dreams will most certainly be crushed. But if you're fortunate enough to hear your songs on the radio or see your CDs sold in stores, it gets to be like a drug . . . you want more."

—**Phil Roy**
Singer-songwriter

CLOTHES MAKE THE BAND

"Recognize that it's okay to dress in a special way when you're on stage. Not everyone is in a jam band or can get away with a dirty t-shirt, looking as if they've mixed-up sound check with show time. There's little credibility gained by dressing like a slacker—at least if you want fans to pay good money to keep coming to see you perform. Too many artists have a "whatever I'm wearing is okay" look when they go on stage. Look: it's competitive and there's lots of entertainment vying for the audience's dollar. Give them something (in addition to your great music) to indicate that you are special and that you do, in fact, possess that power. Let them take that visual home and store it for the next time you come around. If you think this is trivial and so uncool, think about some of the best shows you've ever seen. Have the Stones always had a wardrobe? Does the Dave Matthews Band? U2? Norah Jones? Eminem? Jay-Z? Sloppy chic might work in a club but it does not in larger venues. Start on it now."

—Sean Coakley
Founder, Songlines LTD (music marketing and promotion)

Vivek Tiwary

Starpolish.com Advice Columnist

(For the full article, visit http://www.starpolish.com/advice/article.asp?id=18.

For other great articles, visit http://www.starpolish.com/advice.)

I'm sure you've heard it said that no one can possibly care more about an artist's career than the artist himself/herself. I believe that's true, and that's why—and many others in the music industry may disagree with me here—I am firmly of the opinion that managers should be considered as and act like a member of the band (or a partner if you are a solo artist), and not just a business appendage. A good artist manager is like a good baseball manager—a member of the team, as important a player as any of the others, but providing a different role, looking at things from a different, larger-scale picture and perspective, and calling certain broad-stroke shots that the others simply aren't qualified to.

The best artist managers in music history had relationships with their artists in which they truly were like members of the band or partners with the solo artist. And in today's music industry, which is more dominated by business concerns than ever before, this type of relationship is even more crucial. Ironically, however, in today's music industry, this type of relationship has grown increasingly rare. Most people nowadays tend to think of managers as disposable, and artists' careers are similarly expected to be short-lived. I encourage developing artists and young managers to break that mold—enter a relationship where the manager is treated like an integral partner and is expected to stay (or be kept) for the long haul, through thick and thin, in sickness and in health, 'til death do you part. Indeed, a good artist-management pairing is very similar to a successful marriage. I firmly believe that if more managers and artists strove towards this kind of relationship, we would see more successful career artists (i.e. artists that make music for decades) and the general state of music would be more progressive and creative.

"You kind of have to decide what you want to be known for and what you want people to talk about you as—things like that."

—Mason Jennings

"I tell the truth in the songs as I know it and I don't expect people to agree with me. I don't dictate what the songs mean to people, I just sing them as well and as honest as I can. I think it projects itself to people."

—Mindy Smith

BE YOURSELF

"You must have vision and a sense of self. That's the stuff that makes you the artist that you are, not an imitator, not a cookie-cutter carbon copy of whoever your favorite artist is at the time. How many Eddie Vedder clones came out of the grunge movement? How many young, earnest Dylanesque songwriters honestly need to get past Bob Dylan affectation? Yes, imitation is the highest form of flattery, but there is a reason why Dylan is so successful and attractive to so many—it's because he's Bob Dylan, he's not trying to be anyone else (except for his early infatuation with Woody Guthrie, a step young Zimmerman probably had to take. Point is he outgrew it!). Look within, live deeply, understand your vision of the world, and draw songs from that well. Please, the world doesn't need another Ani DiFranco knock off. Ani is a staggering genius of a songwriter. No one else can be her but her. The world needs you to be YOU!"

—John Francis
Singer-songwriter

John Ondrasik

Creative force behind the platinum award-winning band Five For Fighting

Q&A

1. What would you say are the three or four most important things a young musician should focus on when they are just starting out?

Songwriters should always write a lot of songs. I cringe when I hear of artists shopping the same three songs for two years. Along with writing hundreds of songs, record everything. Even a piano/vocal or guitar/vocal can tell you a lot about your songs when you listen back, perspective is crucial. Finally, and perhaps the hardest, play gigs! Having an audience will allow you to grow as a writer, musician, and performer. Listen to great songwriters and don't obsess on the business aspect, it's music and one of the most honorable of professions.

2. What's the most difficult part of the business of music and what do you suggest musicians should learn about in maintaining control of their careers?

Like any business relationships, work ethic and professionalism can be the difference in commercial success. It may seem strange in the context of rock and roll but promoting a record and working within the label entails a huge amount of time and energy. It's important to hire people around you who have the same ethic and passion that you do for your music. You may find yourself in a position where you have to make several artistic decisions a day, at that point trust your gut; I've learned some hard lessons in not doing so.

3. What advice would you give musicians to learn to cope with both positive and negative feedback they get from fans and music critics?

I would say therapy, and that's only half a joke. With something as personal as your music and the nature of the media it can be a brutal awakening. One bad review makes you forget 10 good ones. . . . Some artists never read or acknowledge any reviews positive or negative. Still, the worst songwriter to ever take the stage and sing his/her own song has more balls than the most darling of critics; don't let it consume you whether loved or ridiculed (and you'll get both).

4. What personal qualities do you need to be a musician?

Humility, arrogance, perseverance, passion, insecurity, confidence, selflessness, selfishness, patience, anger, ego and one hell of a sense of humor.

5. What do you draw inspiration from?

You always should be on the lookout for inspiration. A song is usually in front of you if you look hard enough. Inspiration is different for everyone. It may come in personal experience, a cultural viewpoint, a sentiment, a story, a tragedy, a triumph. It also may come through another's eyes. Many of my songs come out of conversations I have with my children, my friends, and people I meet. Authors and films can be inspiring. For me it's easier to find inspiration in the darker aspects of one's emotional state than the lighter.

6. What kind of process would you suggest a musician take in writing songs?

I like to just roll tape (or bytes) when I'm writing so I don't lose the flow in an idea. The work ethic comes into play in going back and listening to dozens of hours of such dabbling to find that one gem. Also experiment, if you are a multi-instrumentalist you'll find different songs come from different tools. I write on both guitar and piano for different colors. Try writing a lyric first before you even look for melody. Also concept is key, a great concept is the key to a great song. The rest is just writing 100 verses till you get the three that work.

7. How do you cope—and what advice would you give a young musician in coping—with a setback in your career?

I spent two years making my first record and the record

label closed the week it came out. It never saw the light of day. Most bands experience something similar on their road. It can be devastating and words won't ease the pain. That's where the ego and denial comes in to keep doing it. It takes a unique personality to survive the rejection and disappointments . . . and it always exists no matter what level of "success" you might attain.

Vivek Tiwary

Starpolish.com Advice Columnist

(For the full article, visit http://www.starpolish.com/advice/article.asp?id=31
For other great articles, visit http://www.starpolish.com/advice.)

Street marketing teams are so important for *all* developing artists, that almost every major label (and many independent ones) develop street teams in-house, responsible for assisting with the marketing of all their new releases. I created the Alternative Marketing Department at Mercury Records and developed and oversaw its Marketing Team for three years. Our reps' efforts were integral in assisting several great bands break through or cross over to platinum-level success, including 311, The Mighty Mighty Bosstones, Cake, and The Cardigans, to name a few.

Many developing artists assume that they will be unsuccessful at putting a dedicated street team together until they have already achieved some degree of success. Not so. You can—and should—start a street team at the very beginning of your career. In fact, that's when you'll need their help the most. Even if your team consists of five reps in your hometown, that's five more people than you had dedicated to your cause before you started the team. If you and your team work hard, you will grow together.

2

INSPIRATION & EXPRESSION

"There's as much danger in thinking you know it all as there is in not following your own muse. . . . There's so much to be learned from what has gone before you."

—Michael McDonald

Musicians draw inspiration from a variety of sources, some obvious and some not. And what inspires you comes out in your expression as a musician.

Experiencing art, watching a movie, reading a book, walking through a park on a sunny day, or taking a trip to Europe are all activities that are bound to have some impact on your creativity. Some musicians thrive on chaos and pushing their lives to the edge. Other musicians find inspiration in the deepest, most personal and intense emotions that we all experience.

One great piece of advice is to keep a written record of the things that inspire you. Many songwriters write their best after undergoing some very intense emotional experience, like a breakup or a loss of something important. Musicians often go back to their notebooks (or their collection of napkins with scribbled lines) to turn half-baked ideas into full-blown hits.

The greatest songwriters use their personal inspirations to create songs that have universal appeal. This is one of the most challenging aspects of songwriting. As you read the words here, remember one important thing: there is no such thing as inspiration pixie dust. Inspiration won't come magically. Inspiration is often surprising and may hit you when least expected. But one thing remains a constant: you will never be short on inspiration if you get out and experience life and all kinds of people.

BROADEN YOUR HORIZONS

"Listen to underground music. There is a wealth of ideas and diversity in comparison to the mainstream.

Realize that many, if not most, of your heroes were inspired by artists who achieved far less than *they* did in terms of success.

Seek out music that requires an 'acquired taste.' If you hear something that is odd or jarring on first listen, figure out why and learn to embrace those qualities.

Study music. Every day I wish I did.

Learn vocal exercises, and do them regularly.

Learn to accept your voice. Don't try to sing like someone else.

If you are particularly influenced by a current band, find out who they listened to when they were your age and buy as much of that music as you can."

—**Brian McTear**
Producer and member of the band, Bitter Bitter Weeks

"The only really useful stuff that any artist or human being ever finally ended up with is what was true for him."

—Chick Corea

"I always just follow my joy. Seek what inspires you."

—Oteil Burbridge

A WORLD OF INSPIRATION

"I draw inspiration from the vast cacophony of human beings on this planet. The stories of immigrants, working-class heroes, children, rich, poor, movers and shakers, war veterans, the disillusioned, the empowered, the town criers, those who practice what they preach, the homeless, the outcast, the outsider, the insider who feels like an outsider, the prisoner, the desolate, the immaculate, the mystics and the healers, the soldiers, the peacemakers . . . the darkness, the light, the sorrow, the joy."

— **John Francis**
Singer-songwriter

Jennifer Lasker

President of Lasker Management, representing artists and record producers

For any new artist, I would suggest the following:

Work to perfect your live show. Nobody can take a great live performance away from you.

Build regionally and be proactive in your community.

Play, Play, Play.

Swap gigs with other local/regional bands whose music you respect.

Focus 90 percent of your energies on the art, and 10 percent on marketing. Focusing too much on the "business" will kill the art.

If you get a manager, booking agent and/or record label on board, DON'T STOP working to move your career forward on your own. Don't get lazy or complacent and expect things to happen without your own hard work.

Keep ownership of your master [recordings] and publishing for as long as possible.

"I don't know what it is that makes a song happen, I have really no idea, there's no form to it as far as I'm concerned."

—Mark Knopfler

"In moments when you're not totally inspired, you can translate your thoughts and feelings into words and music."

—Aimee Mann

> "I have a piano in my kitchen;
> I do a lot of writing and cooking
> and drinking."
>
> —Jamie Cullum

> "Music is everything to me
> short of breathing. Music also
> has a role to lift you up—not
> to be escapist but to take you
> out of misery."
>
> —Allen Toussaint

John Francis

Anyone can be a musician, if it simply means playing songs here and there, you know, an occasional gig; a hobbyist. But to rise above the crowd and become an established recording and performing artist it takes tenacity, perseverance, patience, an ironclad work ethic, a sense of self, vision, and sacrifice. Quentin Tarentino said, and I'm paraphrasing, "It's all about who wants it the most, and who's willing to work the hardest for it." That's tenacity, work ethic, perseverance, and patience.

If you're good, I mean truly talented, congratulations, that's the easy part. There may be 50 other artists out there who are just as talented, and who have what they like to call 'the whole package.' (Meaning good songs, good voice, good live show, all coming out of an above-average-looking person.) What will separate the ones who garner success from the other 47 artists of that 50 who won't? It's the ones who want it the most, and who are willing to work the hardest for it. Congratulations, you have chosen perhaps the hardest career path of them all, besides maybe coal mining. But, if you're anything like me or a lot of my friends and colleagues, you really have no choice.

WHAT'S YOUR INSPIRATION?

"Inspiration is different for everyone. It may come in personal experience, a cultural viewpoint, a sentiment, a story, a tragedy, a triumph. It also may come through another's eyes. Many of my songs come out of conversations I have with my children, my friends, and people I meet. Authors and films can be inspiring. For me it's easier to find inspiration in the darker aspects of one's emotional state than the lighter."

—**John Ondrasik**
Five For Fighting

ON ORIGINALITY

"What I look for is originality, something that sets an artist or their work apart from the usual. But the typical bar is looking for a band that does covers, and record companies are always calling radio people saying that their new artist sounds 'just like so-and-so' or the like. There is no figuring why some acts 'make it' or not, why some songs become hits, even after they may have flopped previously. A cover band may please the bar crowd, but, sandwiched between two solid originals on the radio, not so much. So, while doing the current trend is useful for getting work, I think some real originality is the thing. Let your mind go wild, see what comes from that."

—Jonny Meister
Host of *The Blues Show* on WXPN-FM in Philadelphia

THE KEYS TO THE KINGDOM

First, love your decision to be in this business and understand this IS a business.

Enjoy yourself. If you aren't having a good time and making friends, this journey might not be for you.

Hang out with the music community—this is networking!

Master the performance. Get in front of the crowd at the bar and sing and keep singing even if no one is listening— someday they will hear you!

Keep a daily journal—it will help you write songs that relate to life.

Put a good support system in place.

Make careful decisions. Don't rush into any deals that seem too good to be true.

Have a firm, confident handshake! That handshake is sometimes your first impression—make it a good one!

—Helen Leicht
WXPN-FM mid-day host, Philadelphia

"You never know what can happen; very soon it became obvious that we had captured something and it had started to write its own story before our very eyes."

—David Gray

"We challenge each other in a really positive way."

—Dave Matthews

> "To me, blues is about grace
> in the face of diversity."
>
> —Sonny Landreth

> "I don't do what I do because
> I plan it, or I think about it.
> The moment before I play,
> I hear it, and feel it."
>
> —Joe Sample

Mutlu

The three most important parts of making music for me are learning how to be in the moment, having fun, and surrounding myself with as many positive, inspiring people as possible. It is important for me whether I'm writing, recording or onstage to push myself to be as immersed in what I am doing as I can. It's not always easy because the business and just life in general can be distracting. As much as possible I try to lose myself in the process.

Although there can be a lot of distractions it's important to find ways to connect to the joy of making music. It is important to stay on top of the business. Labels, managers and agents all play important roles in helping artists achieve their goals. From time to time, however, I find myself too caught up with the business and the desire of "making it." When that happens I try to find ways to take a step back and reconnect to why I do this in the first place. Humor (performing and writing silly songs) sometimes helps me not take it all too seriously.

Once you start getting some opportunities and having some success the expectations and pressure can rise. I try to remind myself from time to time that this can be an unpredictable and fickle business. Everyone inevitably experiences some level of frustration and disappointment. Someone once told me that if you've got talent and a good work ethic that the last key ingredient is persistence. Regardless of what happens, if you focus on being the best you can be you will be successful. I try to remind myself that my career shouldn't be about some sort of popularity contest. Music is about expression and bringing people together. If you're able to go out there and connect with people (on whatever level that might be) then you've got what it takes.

> "I was fortunate because
> I had great teachers."
>
> —Sonny Landreth

> "Follow your inspiration. And if
> you feel like it's (music) what
> you want to do, don't let anybody
> stop you. Dream big."
>
> —Oteil Burbridge

David Poe

My advice? Play! Play and play and play and play.

What else?

Read. Books and stuff. It inspires lyrics, and words are important. (No matter what your drummer tells you.)

Own your songs—legally, and figuratively.

Write songs constantly, but also, learn and perform songs written by other people. Especially the Beatles. It's the best primer.

Learn to record your work.

Be friends with other bands, and play with other musicians whenever you can. Despite the proliferation of "Battle of the Bands" scenarios, music is not a competition. In many ways, playing music is the opposite of playing sports—and eminently cooler.

Once on tour in Florence, Italy, I visited the de Medici family's gallery and was amazed at how many exquisite masterworks were exhibited there by various amazing painters whom I HAD NEVER HEARD OF. The lesson here for creatives is to work without superimposing any expectation of wealth and/or fame on their process. Music is not generally a vehicle to celebrity—and when it's treated as such, the cultural contribution is nil and the songs are invariably bad (except in the case of The Monkees.) Remember that most folks don't know who wrote "Somewhere Over The Rainbow," nor the name of the guy who invented the refrigerator. But clearly their work is valuable, and survives.

"I make music because, since I was two-and-a-half and discovered the piano, that's all I've ever wanted to do. And I make music because I think it helps the world keep chaos at bay."

—Janis Ian

"It's important for me not to sit still; I don't like to do the same thing all the time. I think it's also an ongoing search to find something like perfection—it's worth looking for."

—Bruce Cockburn

CHALLENGE YOURSELF

"Challenge yourself, on a daily basis, to be better. Better at songwriting, performing, recording—everything you do. Accept and be proud of what you do well, but focus on what you can do better. Even when you're exceeding your initial expectations, reflect on what's gone both wrong and right, and figure out how you can improve it. You'll never write the perfect song, you'll never do the perfect show and you'll never make the perfect record. But you'll be a hell of a lot more satisfied and have a boatload more fun—and probably have greater success—if you never allow complacency to settle in."

—Jack Barton
Senior Director, *Friday Morning Quarterback*

Gran Bel Fisher

Singer-songwriter

To sum up what I've learned in the music business is to separate that very term: "music, business."

A lot of us could sit in a dark room for the rest of our lives and play music to ourselves and be content. But a point comes when you see a listener react and then something changes. You realize that there's a chance that something so selfish to you has the power to inspire others and how could you not take that gamble and it is just that, a gamble.

There is nothing worse than having someone say they don't like a song you wrote about your love of a lifetime but nothing better than someone else saying that that same song saved his or her marriage.

Be true to yourself and surround yourself with people that challenge you daily; life's too easy to not be challenged. Art and commerce is a hard thing to balance but stepping out of that dark room is the first step. Sacrifice; and most of all— rock 'n' roll.

"I make music for self-expression. It's a good way for me to channel anger and frustration. In my daily life I'm a quiet unassuming person, but when I get up on stage or when I'm sitting down writing a song, I don't have any fear. I'm able to say things that in real life I can't say."

—Amy Rigby

"I make music because I have something to say, to offer. I've trained my artistic antenna to pick up on issues rather than just relationships and what happens in the bedroom. I write about those, but I occasionally look out the window and wonder what's happening in the world."

—Billy Bragg

Melody Gardot

Q&A

1. What kinds of advice were you given when you were first starting out and who gave it to you?

"Don't be afraid of rejection." I remember a teacher talking about Charles Schulz and how he had to submit his work again and again before anyone would even look at his comics. I thought it was incredible because his work was witty and adorable, and for anyone to reject it seemed absurd. Without his relentlessness though, his work would never have been published. Such is the same in music. If you stop trying because someone rejects what you have done, you'll never know if you could have made a difference with your music. You have to face rejection again and again especially in the music industry because so much of what is "good" or "bad" is merely opinions. Embrace rejection and hold on to hope no matter what happens.

2. What would you say are the three or four most important things a young musician should focus on when they are just

starting out?

1. The writing of the songs

2. The quality/essence of the recording (lo-fi is okay if done right)

3. The quality of the live performance

If one area is weaker than the other, work on it. Most importantly work on the live show. If you can't deliver live, it's likely you will have a hard time developing a following in your area.

3. What's the most difficult part of the business of music and what do you suggest musicians should learn about in maintaining control of their careers?

Do not become a musician if you want to make money right away. Handling a career is just like handling a small business: there are risks and rewards and more likely than not you'll spend more than you make in the beginning. You'll need a support system financially whether it's someone who believes in your music and wants to help, no strings attached, or someone who is willing to invest and wait to get their money back. Make sure you have someone to lean on.

Once you get your footing, have a clear idea of what you want to say as a musician. Your words are powerful and every compromise you make changes the way those words affect other people. Before you go chasing after a recording contract to "make it big," it helps to know exactly where you stand artistically and morally. Anyone can come along offering you the world but it might cost you more than you think if you're not prepared.

Ultimately, if you are sure of what you want, you can always maintain control of your career because you'll know in your heart what's "compromise" and what's "out of the question."

4. What advice would you give musicians to learn to cope with both positive and negative feedback they get from fans and music critics?

Everyone has an opinion about everything. Just because someone who comes to your shows feels that your music is fantastic, that doesn't mean that the hot critics in LA are going to go gaga for your work. If you remember that opinions are just that—individual ideas and not fact—you'll be prepared for any reviews that come your way. Don't let a little criticism make or break you. Understand that you can't please everyone, but you'll succeed if at the end of the day, you have pleased yourself.

5. What are the unexpected consequences of being a musician and what would you tell a young artist to be on the look out for or be aware of?

As a musician you are constantly bombarded with opportunities. Some are good and some are not so worthwhile. If you can find a mentor, or someone you trust, check with them and see what they think about what you are being offered. Everything from gigs to record contracts are subject to misleading information, and if you have another person who can take a look at the opportunity it helps to see through some of the nonsense that you might overlook out of excitement.

Be wary of people who make you promises to "make you a star" or "the next big thing." In particular, be very careful not to sign agreements that you haven't had looked over by a professional. In this business very few people are looking out for your best interest. It's very easy for someone to make it seem like they are helping you, or giving you an amazing opportunity, when in reality there is something tricky in the fine print.

There is an organization in Philadelphia called the PVLA (Philadelphia Volunteer Lawyers for the Arts). If you can't get a lawyer to look over a contract, or you don't know anyone, call them and they can help you.

6. What has happened to your career that you did not expect from this kind of "job"?

From the music, came the opportunity to connect with people in ways I never would have imagined. I find e-mails daily with strangers who share their experience and it's incredibly touching. You never realize how strong your voice can be until you give it a chance to be heard.

7. Being in the studio by yourself and being on stage in front of people are two different things. What advice would you give to a musician first playing out in public?

Treat the audience just like you treat your friends. Talk to them, perform to them, make them feel warm and welcome. If you play to your shoes or say very little while on stage, you miss an opportunity to relate to them. More than anything, don't stress over little things like mistakes in your playing or your voice cracking, or messing up a verse; you're human. People know that.

I'll never forget I started a song and had the guitar in the wrong tuning! Talk about embarrassing! I had to start over after playing for about 30 seconds! And you know what? I made a joke about it and laughed at myself on stage and before you knew it the whole place was laughing too. We shared an embarrassing moment, but they didn't hold it against me. If anything it just reaffirms that you're just a regular person like them.

8. How do you cope—and what advice would you give a young musician in coping—with a setback in your career?

The best thing you can hope for is continued growth. If you have a bad show, and something goes wrong, go home and review it. Talk to a few friends and figure out what you could have done differently. Be humble and learn from your mistakes. If you can learn something from every show that you do, you will become great in no time.

And hey, if Ashlee Simpson can do a hoedown on SNL, get caught lip synching, and STILL have a career, what could you possibly do that would ruin yours? Time heals everything.

If you screw up royally at a show, just make a point never to do it again. We all have to start somewhere and no matter who you are, it's a long climb to the top.

9. Being a musician must put some strain on personal relationships. What things should musicians just starting out be aware of and what kinds of problems should they anticipate?

I have a personal rule of never dating another musician. Why? There's no time for either party to see each other. Being a musician, especially a solo artist takes a great deal of time and effort. And until you are secure in your career, it's a sacrifice of both time and energy to have a serious relationship with another person.

If you are fortunate enough to find someone who understands what your goals are and how much dedication you have, you can make it work. And even if for some reason it doesn't work out, you just got yourself some new material for your record!

"Always make music for the right reasons. If you write songs and perform for the express intention to get a record deal, you're setting yourself up for a fall. Express yourself—don't exploit yourself—with your music. If you write and perform to fulfill *yourself*, you'll always succeed to some degree."

—Dan Reed

"I make music because it's something that helps me to get emotions out in a positive way. And so if I am feeling frustrated about something that is happening in a personal relationship or if I'm feeling angry about something I just read in the newspaper I will write a song about it."

—Michael Franti

"When you're making music you have to do what feels right, and you gotta follow your heart . . . why do it if you're not going to do that? You don't want to follow some textbook."

—Neil Young

"Our educational system should be how to develop the skills to interpret what we are hearing and what we are feeling . . . not to sit and play what we have been taught."

—Joe Sample

Scot Sax

Multi-instrumentalist and former member of the band Wanderlust

Q&A

1. What kinds of advice were you given when you were first starting out and who gave it to you?

All I remember hearing when I was a kid was that the chances of making it were a million-to-one. I think that my family saw in my eyes that there was no other thing I wanted to do other than play music and it scared them. The "million-to-one" thing never had any impact on me.

2. What would you say are the three or four most important things a young musician should focus on when they are just starting out?

Play with people you like to be with as opposed to the hotshots with the expensive equipment. Don't be shy about your talent, play for as many people as you can. Then when you get on stage in front of strangers at clubs you'll be used to being "on the spot" so to speak and your playing and vibe will be very natural. Also, getting feedback on your playing/writing is very important. You can learn a little from everyone and it all adds up to you being the best musician you can be. Plus, you'll learn how to take criticism.

3. What's the most difficult part of the business of music and what do you suggest musicians should learn about in maintaining control of their careers?

Sometimes the word "contract" sounds like the word "success" to a young musician.

Keep in mind that NOT having a record contract can be the best thing in the world.

These days, there is not and should not be any real rush to sign a record contract before you get a chance to try to see how far you can get without one. It's just music—music, fans and word of mouth when you get right down to it. So, make the music, get it heard any way you can (give out CDs, play shows . . . play everywhere) and always mean it.

4. What advice would you give musicians to learn to cope with both positive and negative feedback they get from fans and music critics?

Even the Beatles have people that hate their music (very hard to understand but true).

Try hard to not take it as a personal stab at you. It's a very opinionated thing, music. Get used to it ASAP.

5. What advice do you have for being on the road and balancing the need for personal time and creative time?

Spend the money for your own hotel room once in a while. Get away from the guys. Let them go out to eat and stay in your room and write. Without creativity, the road can be like playing on a sports team. Keep the music flowing in your head. Partying is great, but if you take a long break from being creative it will show. Use it or lose it, as they say.

6. What are the unexpected consequences of being a musician and what would you tell a young artist to be on the lookout for or be aware of?

Drunk people telling you that you are amazing is usually just drunk people telling you that you are amazing. Don't get addicted to praise when the alcohol is flowing. If you know you sucked, you probably sucked. Think about your performance the next day and do it better the next time you play. Be hard on yourself while still having fun. It's an art worth learning.

7. What personal qualities do you need to be a musician?

Be a good guy. Be cool. Be nice. Be firm. Respect people. Put music first. Being confident in the fact that you are doing something that speaks to you and may not be what everyone else is doing, stylistically or whatever, is the key to your happiness and probably success.

8. What are three things you like best about being a musician?

It's an extension of who I am so I always know what's happening in my life by recording and writing it as I go. I always feel like me . . . like I did when I was little. I didn't "grow up" in a way and that suits me just fine. Plenty of time for that anyway. One of my very fave things about being a musician has always been the freedom to wear whatever I want. Never having to fit in to something. Of course there are some musicians that wind up wearing what they "think" is what a musician is supposed to wear and that's really just as bad and conformist-like as a suit and tie in an office.

9. What has happened to your career that you did not expect from this kind of "job"?

I never had any desire really to write songs for other people because I have always written for myself. But that's what I do a lot of these days and it has widened my world big time as far as meeting people, making many friends from around the world and having the thrill of somebody liking your song so much they want to sing it.

10. What do you draw inspiration from?

Things I hear people say, things I hear myself say. I started listening to some of the funny shit I say sometimes and put it into my songs. The first time I did this was "hello to your mother, your brother, significant other." I would start my conversation like that when I would call my buddy and fellow musician friend Mark. I decided to open a song with that, and that song went on to be the most successful song up to that point for me. Wound up in the *American Pie* movie.

11. What kind of process would you suggest a musician take in writing songs?

Don't try to write "really good lyrics." Just write the way you talk and feel. Don't try to be a poet on every line.

"I realized it isn't like the *Wizard of Oz* guy behind the curtain; people are making stuff happen everywhere. It comes down to individuals more than I thought it ever did . . . it's just people running the show."

—Sarah Harmer

"Music is its own reward . . . it will nourish your soul whether or not you become a platinum selling artist."

—Sting

"I certainly understand that we're all trying to make a living, but I'm not thinking about that when I'm making music. And if that's your sole motivation, it's going to reflect that narcissistic greed and you're going to hear it in the music."

—Aimee Mann

"It is important to stay on top of the business. Labels, managers, agents, etc. all play important roles in helping artists achieve their goals. From time to time, however, I find myself too caught up with the business and the desire of 'making it.' When that happens, I try to find ways to take a step back and reconnect to why I do this in the first place."

—Mutlu

"When you realize that music is something you want to do with your life and you're not in the pursuit of fame or money in regards to that music, it's really just the pursuit of a vocational life as a musician."

—KT Tunstall

"Let the melody sing! The melody, the harmony, and the rhythm . . . I love them all!"

—Joe Sample

3

WRITING & PERFORMING

"There is nothing worse than having someone say they don't like a song you wrote about your love of a lifetime, but nothing better tha[n] someone else saying that that same song saved his or her marriage."

—Gran Bel Fisher

Musicians all seem to agree on at least two Golden Ground Rules. They are: Play, play, play. And write, write, write.

Performing on a regular basis and constantly writing songs are crucial to your development as a musician. There is both an art and a science to writing and performing. The science is in how you use the technology available to advance your goals as a musician. The art is the creative process that requires discipline and constant care and work and improvement.

A musician once told me that writing songs and making albums are invitations to fans to come see you perform. Then, once you get fans to your show, you must dazzle them. You must take them to a place that transcends the recorded work if you want them to come back to see you play. This is what building a following is about. And many musicians count on touring as their main source of making money. They may sell albums at their gigs, but when word spreads about the performance, that's the kind of buzz that draws others in.

Ultimately, writing and performing is at the core of your "job" as a musician. There are many facets of being a musician that you will need to pay attention to, but you should pay closest attention to the songs, to the recording, and to performing them with all you've got.

Brian Seymour

Writing when you are blocked is a paradox: the only cure is to write your way out. When I hit a wall, I think of Bob Dylan, who says that when a song just doesn't feel right he changes the key. I try this often. If that doesn't work I try writing on another instrument or even writing without an instrument. Extreme therapy for me is taking a long walk in the city until I've shaped a clear memorable melody or lyric. If all else fails, I try to seek the source of what's holding me back. Based on my experience, songwriters might watch for these quagmires that can lead to writer's block:

Underwhelming an industry somebody that you waited years to impress.

Remedy: Put it down to wrong place-wrong time and channel your frustration into writing your best song.

Overcomplicating things, trying too hard to make the song precious.

Remedy: Simplify, play the melody with one finger and rebuild from there.

Believing that you are Keith Richards and bouncing sleepless in the studio espressoed to high heaven, or worse.

Remedy: Sleep, eat at least one meal that doesn't come in a box, and try cleaning up for a few days to seek clarity.

Running on empty: The ideas just aren't flowing.

Remedy: Read a book, see a great film, listen to music on someone else's iPod, dare to stretch your mind to a new idea.

"I try to get inside the song. If I can live inside the song, it's going to be a good performance."

—Richard Thompson

"I think a lot of artists overlook how intelligent their audience is and how in tune they are to emotion and honesty, and I think when you embrace them, they're going to want to embrace you."

—Mindy Smith

SMART MONEY

"On a business side, remember to budget. Remember to be wise with your money and not spend it all as soon as you make it because you will run into periods where you have a significant time when things are tight and the work isn't flowing in as much. Just stay as balanced in this area as possible and you'll be okay. I'm not saying to be a miser either because you have to invest in your career to do anything."

—Charlotte Martin
Singer-songwriter

Ari Hest

Singer-songwriter

The ability to record yourself is a skill that every musician these days should have. It's easier than ever now, and with the decline of record sales and the trickle-down effect it has had on the productivity of your average recording studio, it's the natural route for a musician to gravitate towards. Yes, it's cheaper, but as I found out, now you don't have to give up on making a quality recording to save money. That being said, I hadn't tried it till this past summer, and I learned first hand how someone with really poor computer skills (me) can successfully grasp the technology and make it work for him/herself. The result was an EP called *The Green Room Sessions,* all home recordings done in my apartment in Brooklyn.

I didn't set out to make a pristine recording. I just wanted something that sounded like it was professional, honest and raw. All the tracks were recorded and mixed in GarageBand using one sm57 microphone. Aside from the cost of my MacBook laptop, the EP set me back a whopping $300. The mic was $50, the M-Audio "Fast Track" pre-amp and M-Audio two-octave keyboard were the other $250.

I set up shop in a vacant room in my apartment, nothing special about it besides the fact that it was empty and had decent acoustics. Through trial and error, I learned a bit about gain structure and mic placement until I got what I wanted. Once I knew I could record a vocal that sounded good (which initially came as a shock) I was excited to learn how to record guitar, bass, keyboards, and anything else around the house that sounded interesting.

Learning how to record myself made me want to take more into my own hands. I felt encouraged to experiment more, and I started to believe (which I surely didn't before) that I could figure it out myself, and that I didn't need a nice recording studio or a great engineer to record what was in my head. I discovered that home recording is a valuable experience because it forces you to try more on your own, and you, in turn, become more well-rounded.

While I'll stop short of saying that I'll never see the inside of a proper recording studio again, I loved doing this EP at home and since it worked out well, I plan on doing a whole lot more like this. Many musicians I come across don't even give recording themselves any thought (for years, I was one of them). But this experience completely opened my eyes to the possibilities of recording more often and inexpensively. At this stage of the music industry's evolution, I believe it's handy to know how to do as much as you can by yourself, including marketing, touring, and recording.

"There's less nurturing in the modern music industry . . . you need to have a hit and then another hit. It's harder to maintain and sustain a career."

—Sting

"It's a very good idea if you can keep changing and doing different things."

—Warren Zevon

"I was really glad when people started recording my songs because that was really what I wanted to be—a songwriter and I wanted to be good enough so everyone would want to record some of my songs, it started happening and I was very glad to see it."

—Willie Nelson

"It was like a collision of the music and the writing, and the performance just came together when I started writing songs."

—KT Tunstall

Phil Roy

Q&A

1. What kinds of advice were you given when you were first starting out and who gave it to you?

I was 17, just out of high school in my first year at Berklee College of Music. Four students, all guitar majors, paid Pat Metheny $25.00 apiece for a private lesson. What he taught me was nothing about scales, licks or chords. Pat Metheny asked us: "So you're guitar players, what kind of guitar player do you want to be? A jazz, country, studio, slide or blues guitar player? A classical, rock, folk, acoustic or electric guitar player? Because unless you really focus on one skill, someone else will and that person will get your gig."

That day had a profound effect on the course of my career. When I found my love for the craft of songwriting I applied what Metheny said to that. Everything I do in one way or another starts with a song. That has always been the focus of my work.

2. What would you say are the three or four most important things a young musician should focus on when they are just starting out?

1. Get extremely proficient on your chosen instrument. You have to put in the time, there's no way around it. Study and practice.

2. Put a band together. Music is to be communicated and shared. Find people at your own skill level or better. Learn to collaborate. It's essential.

3. Learn other people's songs and licks and adapt their artistry to what you can offer. Play lots and lots of styles.

4. Listen to music, a lot of music.

3. What's the most difficult part of the business of music and what do you suggest musicians should learn about maintaining control of their careers?

At the age of 21, I signed my first record deal and became a Warner Brothers recording artist. Over the past 25 years I've had enough record deals, production deals and publishing deals to fill a chapter of this book. Realize this. The music business is a minefield filled with lies, deceit and uncertainty. You have to be skilled, lucky or a combination of both. Your dreams will most certainly be crushed. But if you're fortunate enough to hear your songs on the radio or see your CDs sold in stores it gets to be like a drug . . . you want more. It's hard to stop. In the beginning your career will be as good as the people who surround you both creatively and professionally. Surround yourself with people who are enthusiastic about what you do. It helps if someone believes in you enough to want to spend money on your talents. In the end you better make a great record, write a "hit" song, or be extremely good-looking like me.

4. What advice would you give musicians to learn to cope with both positive and negative feedback they get from fans and music critics?

Dealing with positive feedback doesn't really have too many downsides unless people are just 'bullshitting' you and are not telling you the truth about how they really feel about your music. In regards to negative feedback, get used to rejection, get used to the word "no," you better have thick skin. If you're good, there is a "yes" out there that can change your life. If all you're getting is negative feedback for years and years, maybe you have to look at the content of your music and stop blaming everyone else.

5. What advice do you have for being on the road and balancing the need for personal time and creative time?

I never spent a lot of time on the road. I mostly made a living writing and recording in Los Angeles. Now that I live in Philadelphia, I'm touring more and it does have some elements that can put stress on your personal life. Find a girl or guy that "gets" the lifestyle if you're going to have a relationship/marriage.

Keep a tape recorder or notepad around for ideas when you're driving, they fade away as fast as the lines on the highway go by.

6. What are the unexpected consequences of being a musician and what would you tell a young artist to be on the lookout for or be aware of?

You will have to accept the uncertainty of your path. It's not for everyone. Be aware, a small, small percentage of very talented people actually get to make a living playing and writing original music. If you ever earn a decent sum of money from a deal, buy a house. At least you'll always have a place to live.

7. What personal qualities do you need to be a musician?

Perseverance and a point of view.

8. What are three things you like best about being a musician?

The hours, the audience, royalty checks.

9. What has happened to your career that you did not expect from this kind of "job"?

I made life long friends and traveled the world.

10. Being in the studio by yourself and being on stage in front of people are two different things. What advice would you give to a musician first playing out in public?

Make sure you're in tune.

11. What was your first public performance like?

I was 13 at my junior high school dance, in the cafeteria playing Hendrix songs, with my guitar slung behind my neck, having a blast.

12. If you have ever had a "writer's block" what kind of things did you do to get out of it?

I'd go to where lots of people congregate, parks, malls, sit on a bus; that helps me. Also there's nothing quite like a deadline.

13. What do you draw inspiration from?

Desperation and beauty. Struggle and redemption.

14. What kind of process would you suggest a musician take in writing songs?

For me narrative is king. Melody, rhythm and feel are the king's best friends. This advice is useless if you're into writing instrumental music or dance tracks for clubs.

15. How do you cope—and what advice would you give a young musician in coping—with a setback in your career?

Make another record. Do another show. Some are better than others, that's the way it goes.

"When I don't get a warm audience, I try to win them over with my charm."

—Mindy Smith

"When I see live music I want to see more energy, something about the person and what they're about."

—Mason Jennings

Birdie Busch

Singer-songwriter

Q&A

1. What are the unexpected consequences of being a musician and what would you tell a young artist to be on the lookout for or be aware of?

I think something that I have witnessed and experienced is the consequence of losing perspective on what is important in your life. This is something that many people, musicians or not, experience. Music, especially when starting out and trying to just get out there and do your thing, can become consuming, taking you from the life and relationships that inspired you in the first place. I would tell folks to just be aware of balancing the two and to not forget that although the quest for the song is beautiful, sacrificing good things in your life, like love and friendship, makes it feel less fruitful in the end.

2. What personal qualities do you need to be a musician?

Fearlessness, conviction, openness, patience, ability to withstand disappointment, adaptability beyond belief, ability to sleep on hard floors, work easily with others, withstand extreme environments, and have the ability to deflect weird music biz types and attract good ones. The ability to be okay with whatever while simultaneously not compromising your art. Basically try and be superhuman and completely human at the same time.

3. What are three things you like best about being a musician?

1. That I really love what I set out to do.

2. That I have met so many people who love what they do in the process.

3. That this love creates this boundless magical energy. I can't imagine doing something I don't love to do. I think this is something that creates such a fascination with musicians. That love is like a force field that you step into when in the presence of that love.

"*For us, writing songs . . . there's a lot of experimentation.*"

—Guster

"**The songs grow out of the lyrics.**"

—Trey Anastasio

"I hold this ethic that it's about the music, it's about making good music."

—KT Tunstall

EDIT YOURSELF

"I think an indispensable piece of advice for any artist—and a mark of true artistry—is to edit yourself! Take a really hard listen to what you've written or recorded. Ask others to critique it for you (and not just your parents, they're biased). Find some good ears on someone who can be utterly truthful and get constructive feedback, then act on it. The mark of all great artists is their ability to edit what they've created, and the mark of all immature artists is to resist the cutting and reworking that is as important as the impulse to create (a song) in the first place."

—**Michaela Majoun**
WXPN-FM Morning Show Host

Tyler Gibbons

Red Heart the Tickler

Early in high school I was playing with a group in bars and clubs all over New England. (Let me just interject here: I was going to write "when I was a young musician," but the title of your book got me to thinking that every single musician I know is a young musician. My mentor, 25 years my senior, is a young musician, just as I am. We are all students, and should revel in the life-long youthfulness of the endeavor.) Being underage by a longshot, we were pretty excited to be in the 21+ scene, and I think, generally accepted (though perhaps with a certain "aw, look how cute" attitude) by the older crowd.

One cold January day, shining with the thin kind of winter light that has a lot in common with ice, we drove our van up to Brunswick, Maine for a show at a small bar (now happily absent from that New England landscape). The club was average in size, shape, smell (worse, perhaps, in cleanliness), and, notably, two flights of stairs below ground. Halfway into our first number a large contingent of folks from the Brunswick Naval Air Station arrived and loudly requested Black Sabbath. We mumbled something about playing originals and then watched as one sailor dropped about 30 quarters into the room's juke-box and selected three Sabbath albums in a row. In an odd pre-cursor to the recent "mash-up" craze, band and jukebox both blared away, different keys, different tempos, in the same 20 x 40 concrete basement.

Then a pretty decent-sized fight broke out. We were never clear what the provocation was, but there were fists and bodies everywhere: on the bar, dance area, our stage (our corner of the floor, more appropriately), and in both the ladies' and men's rooms. A cymbal stand was broken. We packed up and left, Sabbath's remaining soundtrack and brawl still in high gear.

Half a block into our escape we were pulled over by a cop. We told him about the fight, but he was more focused on his instant distrust (I would say hatred, even) of our van. We unpacked every piece of equipment we owned for him and set it on the side of the road. The cold had turned bone chill-ing. We admired his furry cop-cap and his capacity to frown so consistently. He looked under the seats and floor mats, and in the spare-tire well. Unsatisfied, he shone a flashlight in our faces and questioned, in particular, my right eye, which can wander.

At four in the morning, back on the road, we made a pact together: we love this. This is what we love, not a future of the-aters, green rooms, and drivers. We agreed to be musicians in the present, which meant each night was our experience, not a means to some future experience. We banned our egos. We shook hands. Then we drove the six hours, well into daylight, back home. I think about the pact from time to time, and though I don't know exactly how it's served us, everyone is still making music, which says enough.

"Just keep writing songs. These are words I live by. If you don't believe that your best work is still ahead, you're done. We should all be wary of music biz sharks who offer short-cuts to yesterday's hit sound; what catches is a song that is unique and breaks the form, not one that repeats it."

—Brian Seymour

"In some instances the songs come from all of us—they find their way, we don't have a very structured method to writing songs."

—Dave Matthews

"It took us about a year to sort out how we were going to make the music we wanted to make. In making a record we just knew that we finally had the chance to get our music out to people."

—Keane

Kufie Knotts

Q&A

1. What kinds of advice were you given when you were first starting out and who gave it to you?

The best advice that I first got was to always keep in mind that music is a very unfriendly and at times cutthroat business to be involved with. I was told that if you don't have thick skin, don't even try to be in this business. And always have a backup plan. This advice was given to me by Teddy Pendergrass Sr. and Kenny Gamble.

2. What would you say are the three or four most important things a young musician should focus on when they are just starting out?

The practice of dedication and hard work, confidence and humbleness.

3. What's the most difficult part of the business of music and what do you suggest musicians should learn about in maintaining control of their careers?

The most difficult part is managing your time. Second to that, the business aspect of creating music that is most important to be aware of is obtaining copyrights to creations and making sure all legal aspects of your music are in order.

4. What advice would you give musicians to learn to cope with both positive and negative feedback they get from fans and music critics?

Take all criticism as constructive criticism—and remember that you can't please everyone all the time and criticism should never be taken as a personal attack. It should be used to increase awareness of creative goals and to make changes if you see fit.

5. What advice do you have for being on the road and balancing the need for personal time and creative time?

Don't overload yourself with one particular thing. Balance is a necessity of life, not just music. Balance breeds a healthy state of mind that allows you to be creative.

6. What are the unexpected consequences of being a musician and what would you tell a young artist to be on the look out for or be aware of?

As a young artist you always need to be aware of dishonest people with self-serving motives. These kinds of people tell you anything you want to hear but usually only to get something out of you or from you. Maintain your integrity by keeping your eyes open to this kind of thing and stay aware.

7. What personal qualities do you need to be a musician?

Drive and dedication; honesty and patience.

8. What are three things you like best about being a musician?

The creative process, musical expression and freedom to create one's own style.

9. What has happened to your career that you did not expect from this kind of "job"?

Stress—a lot of it.

10. Being in the studio by yourself and being on stage in front of people are two different things. What advice would you give to a musician first playing out in public?

Self-confidence is the most important part of performing. It is also important to remember that musicians are only human and not every performance will meet your own personal expectations. This is to be expected and should not prevent you from getting back up there any chance you get.

11. If you have ever had a "writer's block" what kind of things did you do to get out of it?

When I have a block I simply don't write. I wait for it to pass because I have found that trying to force it is the worse thing I can do. A little distance can open your creativity in a refreshed direction.

12. What do you draw inspiration from?

Everyday living.

13. What kind of process would you suggest a musician take in writing songs?

I would say when you get "that feeling" you should write it down and don't try to force it any other time.

14. How do you cope—and what advice would you give a young musician in coping—with a setback in your career?

Take it with a grain of salt and remember that there are some things you have no control over and one show does not define a career. Keep positive!

15. Being a musician must put some strain on personal relationships. What things should musicians just starting out be aware of and what kinds of problems should they anticipate?

Your commitment to your art will take up most of your time, so be cautious of who you become involved with on a personal level. Be sure they are not needy for time and attention because most likely you won't be able to offer what they need.

16. What's your favorite thing about being a musician?

The freedom of self-expression.

"Get a good lawyer and don't sign anything without running it by them first. You don't need a big-shot entertainment lawyer at this stage, just a trusted friend of the family who will give you honest (and cheap!) advice."

—Carbon Leaf

"Never ever 'write for the radio.' When you aim for radio play, listeners can tell and usually the music sounds contrived and untrue. Always write what you know and feel and let the chips fall where they may. If radio gets it, great. If not, then you're probably ahead of them. The most lasting music is usually from artists that were *very hard* to get airplay for."

—Sean Coakley

Andy Blackman Hurwitz

Owner/founder, Rope-A-Dope Records

I would have had a totally different opinion 2 to 3 years ago, but now, in 2006, this is what I tell everyone that sends me demos, asks for advice, and wants to know how to "make it":

Fuck the music industry.

Artists today have every possible tool and opportunity they need to be self-contained, self-sustaining entities. Record your music, make your CD, create your Web site and your MySpace spot, play for anyone and everyone, build up your own fan base (one person at a time), develop your music (by all means necessary—that means getting a day job that allows you to pay your bills and practice your art), and don't be waiting around for the magic phone call from the record label, the big-wig manager, or the big-money publisher. Expect nothing from the industry and you won't be disappointed. At the same time, adjust your expectations. You might not ever be living a lifestyle of the rich and famous, or be on MTV or even on the radio. BUT, if you are dedicated to your art, you may very well have the opportunity to be a professional musician, earning a decent living by playing music. And it doesn't get any better than that.

And when doing all of the above, when that magic phone call comes—and it will—well, you'll be psyched, but you won't be pressured to take a shitty deal or sign your life away.

"I have a philosophy when I make a record;
I'm making *a* record, not *THE* record. You
have to remain flexible and make changes."

—Trey Anastasio

*"For me making music is always a collaboration
and I've always co-produced my records with a
great team . . . it really is a collaborative effort.
'Its always heart and soul.'"*

—Bonnie Raitt

"Remember that there are many levels of success.
And each one has it own sets of rules and prices to
pay. Sometimes being a successful local or regional
act will prove to be more rewarding in the long run
than trying to become an international 'star.'"

—John Schoenberger

Nate Reuss

Member of power-pop and rock-
influenced band, The Format

Q&A

1. What kinds of advice were you given when you were first starting out and who gave it to you?

Some friends who owned an indie label that our old band would constantly try to get signed to would tell us "one of the best ways to be successful is to be a great live band and to play as much as possible." We feel like those are words to live by.

2. What would you say are the three or four most important things a young musician should focus on when they are just starting out?

1. Become familiar with your voice or your instrument.

2. Work on songwriting and varying structures.

3. Study music by listening to others.

4. Have fun.

3. What's the most difficult part of the business of music and

what do you suggest musicians should learn about in maintaining control of their careers?

The most difficult part of the business is discovering that it can be a *business*. When we first started the band we thought that we were in charge of writing the music and everyone else was going to make it happen. Really quickly we realized that we have to partake in almost every decision, otherwise people will take advantage of the things you "don't want to know." We feel like the majority of the people we've met in the major label music business have their own agenda . . . and I guess they should—it is the business of making money. So as a musician or artist you have to decide whether you want to play the game or not. Everyone thinks they will be the exception to the rule, but it's rarely ever the case. The best thing to do is be cautious and conscious in all of your business decisions. Make sure you have the right people working for you and even though we'd all like to assume that it's a perfect world where there is no business in making art, it's generally not that way. Pay attention.

4. What advice would you give musicians to learn to cope with both positive and negative feedback they get from fans and music critics?

That depends on what they're in it for. If a musician is making music in an attempt to please everyone then they're most likely in for a letdown. I don't think anyone has the same tastes in everything so you have to get used to the fact that some people like you and others don't. Getting offended usually doesn't help . . . you can't change people's opinions if they don't want to give it a chance.

5. What advice do you have for being on the road and balancing the need for personal time and creative time?

Being creative is the best use of personal time on the road. Just try not to annoy everyone around you.

6. What are the unexpected consequences of being a musician and what would you tell a young artist to be on the look out for or be aware of?

The business will always be the hardest thing to deal with. If you don't care about the business and you're only out to make your art, oblivious of the financial consequence then that's great. But if you want a large amount of people to hear you, that usually takes some time dealing with the business end of things. Just remember the reason you're doing it. And be honest with yourself. It's a struggle, but as long as you stick to your guns it should get you through troubling times.

"Sometimes when we record we don't go in there with an agenda . . . you have a song and it's scripted out to certain people. It's funny when you get five people together in a room . . . a sort of equilibrium establishes itself quite quickly and it's not any conscious thing; it just happens and thankfully in this case it works."

—Radiohead

"Warm sounding people make a warm sounding record."

—Joe Henry

"Something other than a guitar and your voice [will catch a crowd]."

—Old Crow Medicine Show

ON THE ROAD

"I love touring. To me it's the other side of the coin. If you ever think about creating an animal the record is really the test-tube animal. It's got all the bones and all the muscles and the nerves and it's looking at you but on the road that's when you take that animal out and you kind of have it on a leash but you don't know if you can hold on to it. That's when you can see what it can do. That's when the songs become totally real."

—Josh Ritter
Singer-songwriter

> "*To introduce a lot of new material in a concert is difficult—any musician will tell you that.*"

—Elvis Costello

> "Become a health freak when you are on tour. Eat whole foods and wash your hands all the time. Sneak away to warm up your voice before you do a sound check or sing on stage. Get a vocal warm-up recording (the cornier, the better) and use it religiously."

—Brian McTear

Refine your live act and tour a lot both to get better and to find out if the touring life is for you. It's not easy and it's not for everyone. However, it's critical to succeed. If you do this well, and continually grow your live-touring base, you can have a long-term career. Radio play did not come easy or early for some our biggest acts (Dave Matthews, Springsteen etc.) but their live show was not to be denied. These days with the Internet (MySpace, etc.) you have an asset to spread the cult of you that is very powerful to help grow the touring base."

—James Evans
Director of Rock Promotion, Interscope Records

FINDING YOUR STYLE

"You will often hear the advice, 'No matter what you do, try to be as unique as possible.' It is true that if you are original, and you stick to it, *eventually* you will receive recognition in some way, shape or form. The problem is, especially for young artists, it's difficult to know just what to do to be unique. Sometimes the answers come down to very nuts-and-bolts options.

One good example is to learn to step outside the predominant rhythms that exist in the music you listen to. Every genre of music has its typical drum rhythms and strum patterns. Country patterns are country. Punk beats are punk. Emo rhythms are usually noticeably emo. It's easy to recognize when it's not *your* music, but harder to tell when it is.

So if you write punk songs, see what it is like to superimpose everything about them over, say, samba patterns. If you can make it work, people with think you are a genius. Indeed, whole new genres can develop this way."

—Brian McTear
Producer and member of the band, Bitter Bitter Weeks

A MUSICIAN'S LIFE

"I think musicians and artists are outlaws by nature. We are never the normal people. We're the ones who are always standing outside looking in to see how real people behave."

—Janis Ian
Singer-songwriter

The words of wisdom in this chapter come from a WXPN-FM radio series entitled, *A Musician's Life*. In this series—recorded in September and October, 2006—musicians offered first-person narratives about their lives and work as artists.

For the most part, a musician's everyday life looks very different from that of the average person. They sleep strange hours, cobble together odd jobs to stay afloat, live out of suitcases, sacrifice their relationships, and often put their craft above all other things in their lives.

Some of the things these artists were asked include:

What was the biggest sacrifice you ever made for your art?
How do you work with the music industry?
How do you feel about critics and fans?
What are the most remarkable realities of touring?
What is the story behind a specific song?
Have you had any fallout from writing about people
    in your life?
Has your work taken any tolls on your personal life?
How do you deal with writer's block?
Did you grow up wanting to be a musician?
How do you take care of your voice?
How do you take care of your health in this business?

As you'll read here, each of these musicians have their own special place from which they draw their energy. Hopefully their words will in some way help point you towards your deepest and most meaningful well of creativity from which to draw.

BILLY BRAGG

I make music because I have something to say, to offer. I've trained my artistic antenna to pick up on issues rather than just relationships and what happens in the bedroom. I write about those but for most of the songs I write about, I occasionally look out the window and wonder what's happening in the world.

If I didn't become an artist I probably would have been a tank commander, driving a truck in the Army. If I didn't do this job I'd have probably gone mad. I'd be speaking on a street corner somewhere. The urge to communicate would have found its way out.

JANIS IAN

I am a journeyman songwriter and artist. I make music for a lot of different reasons. I make music because that's what I've always done. I make music because since I was two-and-a-half and discovered the piano that's all I've ever wanted to do. And I make music because I think it helps the world keep chaos at bay.

I think musicians and artists are outlaws by nature. We are never the normal people. We're the ones who are always standing outside looking in to see how real people behave. Stella Adler, my acting teacher, used to say, "Trust your talent"—it will be there when you need it. The perspective only comes really with age.

JOSH RITTER

I write rock and roll with lots of words. I make music because it's the thing that feels most natural to me. I think of music as a pipe cleaner . . . it goes in and it scrapes away all the calcite on the rain pipes and lets the water flow freely. Without it I would just jam up. There are places that I hold dear for reasons of music. The Minneapolis airport—for some reason I've written three songs at three different times there. And they've all ended up on records. I've got a spot I go behind the pretzel store when I have long layovers. Leonard Cohen has said if he knew where the good songs came from he'd go there more often and I would suggest the Auntie Anne's pretzel place in the Minneapolis airport. I do a lot of writing on the road but its mostly just picking up ideas and figuring out how they all fit together.

I love touring. To me it's the other side of the coin. If you ever think about creating an animal, the record is really the test tube animal. It's got all the bones and all the muscles and the nerves and it's looking at you but on the road that's when you take that animal out and you kind of have it on a leash but you don't know if you can hold on to it. That's when you can see what it can do. That's when the songs become totally real. And it can go so many different ways. You can just bomb or it can be really transcendent. And from night to night that can change.

I remember when I first told my parents that I was going to be a musician. It was the night before my first big organic chemistry exam and I said I think I want to be a musician, I want to be a songwriter and I don't think I'm going to pass organic chemistry. But I got this plan all worked out—I need four years. It's like four years of being at graduate school. And then we'll see if I can make this work. I started temp working and started begging for gigs and writing songs. And at the end of three years I was able to support myself.

T-BONE BURNETT

I am a musician, a songwriter and music producer. I remember the first time I ever had a musical experience and it was brief and it was small but it was profound for me. I was at a friend's house and there was an old Gibson acoustic guitar leaning against the wall and I walked over and hit the 'E' string on it and it made this boom, made this crazy sound, and I listened to it as the note died away. I listened to it resonate and an addiction began that day . . . an addiction to sound and all the implications of that. It felt like a safe place, like a key to other universes. You know how you shine a light through a ruby and it becomes a laser. I was only 11 at the time and it had a "through the looking glass" effect on me. In fact it has opened up many many universes of sound for me.

When I started making records, when I started making music, I didn't do it to be a performer, I did it to be a songwriter. I was more removed from the audience when I was younger. I was behind a screen of my own insecurity. I suppose it's the goal of religion, I suppose it's the goal of psychiatry, to find or create the observer. So as you go on, I believe you begin to observe yourself more honestly.

SHAWN COLVIN

My music initially—the first couple of records—was extremely autobiographical. In fact I remember the first record, it seemed like I had tried to write catchy songs before that and I was being dishonest with myself and I remember having a moment where I said, "All your mentors are these confessional songwriters. Why aren't you confessing? Come on, pony up." So here it is and I have now gotten to the point where things are still autobiographical but more loosely so. They can become more abstract or I can insert a character and it may be no one that I know or I can become a character that may not obviously be me, but it all comes from my own experience.

You enter into this business of music—the idea is you work hard and you make a record and your dream has come true. I really was that naïve. I wasn't prepared for the promotional aspect of it. I was in the middle of promoting a new record and you basically work all day and work all night and then drive on a bus for the rest of the night and get up and do it again. I remember calling my manager at the time and saying I was at the end of my rope and I wasn't able to do the show that night—I was that tired. And he said the show is the least important moment of the day. It was a seminal moment for me cause I knew that I would never ever agree with that. Ever, ever, ever.

RODNEY CROWELL

As a songwriter, I always try to remind myself that the audience is not having a relationship with me, they're having a relationship with the music and even more specifically with the song. And I try to remind myself that the songs are what it's about; not me. Ego is a tricky business when you find yourself the center of the universe. I spend a lot of time in my life working on my neediness. I don't have to be in front of an audience to be happy, to be fulfilled—but boy, what a privilege to do it.

STEPHEN STILLS

I started out for fun. Then for the chicks. Then for the chicks and the money. Then for the money again, and then for the joy of it. I'm lucky to have had 40 years of this as a present.

MICHAEL FRANTI

I make music because it's something that helps me to get emotions out in a positive way. And so if I am feeling frustrated about something that is happening in a personal relationship or if I'm feeling angry about something I just read in the newspaper I will write a song about it.

When I was a kid I always felt like an outsider. I grew up in a family where I was adopted. The two parents who raised me were Finnish-Americans. My birth mother is Irish, German and French and my birth father is African-American and Seminole Indian. The reason that I later discovered that my mother gave me up for adoption was that she felt that her family would never accept a brown baby. So because of that I have always felt this disconnection in the family I was raised. And my music speaks to that part of each of us which feels like an outsider and wants to feel connected.

LAURA VEIRS

I make music because it in some kind of way links my subconscious life with my conscious life. By combining words and music I can squeeze something beautiful out of this existence, which is full of struggle and trouble, as we all know. Music for me is a bridge between the normal world and a dream world. Finding a good song is an ephemeral sort of slippery thing and you have to be gentle with yourself and with your muses because I think music is out there for us to just grab but you have to be ready for it.

I didn't intend to be a musician when I was littler; I was thinking I would be an airplane pilot or I'd be a trapeze artist or a ballerina—this was like when I was six. When I was in high school I thought I'd be a photographer and when I got to college I met some people who introduced me to underground music and I discovered this whole other world out there. I got introduced to Ani DiFranco and she was influential in helping me think well, 'I can do this'—everyone is capable of being a musician if they want to. I started getting local shows in Seattle, and traveling around the Northwest and playing underground house parties and coffee shops and it was a very slow process over the years. I was frustrated for a while but I tried to find some positives wherever I could.

Even though it was like slow baby steps, I'm grateful for that because I think that if an artist gets too much sudden success that can mess with their head. I feel like it's been a pretty nice climb.

ALEXI MURDOCH

When I was a kid I remember being really drawn to words. In fact I used to fancy that I would sort of write fiction or something, which I still think about every now and then. The music was always there but it was always separate and at some point it was maybe about five years ago where I realized that wow—what I always thought I'd do as a writer of words has merged with this personal thing, attachment that I had to music.

Songs are strange because they sort of come at you. I don't sit down and spend a lot of time working on refining them. It's more like waiting for enough quiet to hear the next part. So the songs that I feel probably closest to are the ones that come though the quickest. There's a song called "Dream about Flying" which just came at me out of nowhere about four o'clock one morning. That's the one that's still teaching me in a way because it seems to have sort of come before my own understanding of it.

I think my song "Orange Sky" is probably just one of those songs that has universal quality because it's so simple really. I mean it was never, fondly enough—it was never really intended as a song. It's just something I'd kind of go off and sing really for myself. The way the song came about was just I got up at a gig and I thought I'd kind of give it a go and the shape that it took at that specific gig was kind of the shape that it was left in and then was recorded. So it just speaks to very simple things that we all feel for each other ultimately when we're kind of quiet enough to remember.

When you're doing something that you feel strongly about, that you feel that you're actually trying to document— something you know and keeping it honest, it's so challenging to do that anyway without having the added burden of trying to make a living, so I think my biggest fear is that it will start to interfere with the creative process. At the same time you know you're talking about maintaining integrity and purity and that in itself can be a really dangerous proposition or self-proposition in a sense because you don't want to become too precious about it and sort of get up on some horse, high or otherwise.

You know I have no answer about any way to do that other than what I'm managing to do for today.

Being recognized physically for something that you do that really has—well I won't say nothing to do with you—but that's not really you, it's definitely something that is happening more and more and it kind of freaks me out a little bit because I don't quite know how to deal with it. We're all trying to rid ourselves of self-consciousness so when you walk into a room and a certain amount of the people in there recognize you, that could really become quite difficult.

AIMEE MANN

When I graduated high school I didn't really know what to do with my life. I had heard about a music school called Berklee College of Music and they had this summer program. My philosophy about pursuing music—because obviously like everybody else you always hear—"oh it's an impossible business and nobody ever makes it"—so I thought, well, I'll learn about music and maybe that will help me know if I have any talent at it and, at the point when I hit a brick wall and realize I'm not any good at it or that I can't go any further, I'll try something else—and I just never really hit that brick wall.

I can't really write a song about something I don't care about. And I don't tend to write songs unless I can somehow relate them to somebody that I care about. I usually kind of picture a character and that character is usually a composite of different people I know but it usually comes out of great compassion and a desire to understand that person.

Sometimes I kind of get on certain topics that I think are particularly interesting. The idea of people and their obsessive behavior, their compulsive behavior, their addictive behavior—to me—that's really fascinating because why people do things that they don't want to do—that's to me a really interesting question and one that's really important to try to answer. I think songwriting is sort of an attempt to solve a conundrum.

I think writer's block for me is pretty circumstance driven. And in retrospect I think the biggest period of writer's block was when I was on a label and just kind of persistently feeling that it was pointless to write songs that you would then play for people at the label who were guaranteed to not like them and they were guaranteed to not like them because they have a totally different agenda about what constitutes a good song cause they're looking for the sure-fire hit which never exists. It's like the Holy Grail. I think to just feel that you're failing over and over is, it's demoralizing and the sensible reaction is to stop beating a dead horse and so I just stopped.

The song that I had in *Melrose Place,* "That's Just What You Are," it wasn't like I was a *Melrose Place* watcher or anything . . . but because radio is so devoted to Top 40 and the Top 40 is kind of the same around the country, the only way to get your music heard anymore is to have something on TV or in movies.

AARON NEVILLE

I believe God put me here to make music. It's been in my bones and my heart since I can remember. My brother Art said I used to stand up in the crib and just make a loud noise like I was singing till I'd fall asleep. Singing has been a medicine to me through the years. It saved my life.

I used to sing my way into the movies, into the basketball games and stuff like that, but I never looked at it as a power. I just thought of it as, "Hey I'm lucky," you know. But I always marveled at other singers, like Nat Cole and Clyde McPhatter and all the doowop groups and the Cowboys and Sam Cooke but I don't put myself up there with Sam. I feel like Sam was the man you know, a teacher to me. I gotta you know use some of his licks. I've recorded "A Change is Gonna Come" three times.

I went to Catholic school and I never knew the words when I was a kid but always in church I'd hear that song "Ave Maria." It would go like a thread through me and just cleanse me you know and through times in my life I'd be sitting in the gutter you know I didn't have a penny or nothing. I could sing that part of the "Ave Maria" and it made me feel rich, so it's brought me through a few trying times.

I was born and raised in New Orleans and I never wanted to leave New Orleans. I used to tell people "man I've been to some beautiful places around the world you know but the most beautiful sight to me is coming in on the plane and looking down and seeing the swamps but I believe the swamps is gonna take it back."

I left before the storm and I got my family out. I been doing that for the last few years because I knew it was coming and I didn't want to get caught. I keep seeing those people in the water and I say, "There go I but for the grace of God." And I been hearing all kind of stories about what happened to those people and there could be some friends of mine that I don't know if they're dead or alive. I run across different musicians from New Orleans and you know they all have the same look. Cause New Orleans guys, you know the Big Easy, you know "oh we can handle that." But nobody could handle this. I talked with Dr. John he said, "Man I was *traumalatized*." It affects you every time you wake up, you know. And they say grieving comes in stages or whatever, you know. I never really sit down and cry but every once in a while I feel tears behind my eyes. I want to feel optimistic but the New Orleans I knew, I know— it's not gonna be back.

CANDI STATON

I make music because it's like my hand. I can't seem to live without it. What I feel inside, I can portray it easily when I'm singing it. Maybe sometimes I'm not as verbal about things but when I sing what I feel I can bring it out and make you understand it in three minutes.

When I was about five years old—our church—we had a special thing on every fifth Sunday in our little country town in Alabama, and this particular day this family brought their daughter and she did a song and she tore the place down, and that's when the idea came to me: I am going to sing. At first I couldn't get a voice out and I just kept praying—my mother taught us how to pray when we were little kids—and I didn't even realize I could sing. And one day I was just humming and I was doing nice little things with my voice that impressed me, and I was like, SHE MAKES HUMMING SOUND . . . ooh that sounds good.

When I first started singing secular music my mother was very disappointed. She was so hurt because she was taught that you know you didn't mix the gospel with the world. She was like, "girl you know I didn't teach you that and I don't like you being in those night clubs." And she was really grieved over that, but she finally, before she died, came to grips with it. You know she wasn't happy but she could live with it.

The music that I started singing put me into a different category which was "Stand by Your Man." I had done like "Old Man Sweetheart" and I had done "For You" and all these kinds of songs you know before. It was that southern soul stuff and when I made "Stand by Your Man" it took me into a whole different category of music. I got nominated for a Grammy. I sold out the Flamingo in Las Vegas. So it removed me from some of the country chitlin' circuit places that I was singing at. It happened again when I did "Young Hearts Run Free." My career has been up and down and up and down. It's never been like one hit after another one. I never experienced that.

I know who I am and I'm not easily inflated. I keep all the clippings out of the New York Times and the variety magazines and put them all in a little book and I put them all away. And I get my vacuum cleaner and I'll start cleaning my house and I'll wash my clothes and I'll think about other things other than music. I'll go and visit my grandbabies and we'll all go out and have dinner together and, I mean, I know where I am.

STEVEN PAGE

I make music because I feel compelled to. I think there's a lot of things I do in my life and some of them I feel they're just part of who I am. I'm a father because I have children and because I love my children. I'm a musician because that's what's inside of me. And I think that sometimes being a musician is just trying to get the music in your head out of your head. I think if I didn't actually make music out loud I'd probably go crazy.

I didn't think I was going to be a musician. I always loved music. I sang in choirs in high school, I always air guitared in front of the mirror. I wrote songs and made tapes with friends and so on but I think I assumed that I would be a writer. I knew Ed Robertson from school. Ed and I were never friends; he was friends with a friend of mine, but then we were working together at a music camp and he was walking around one day with his guitar and he was singing some songs that I had written with another friend of mine. I of course was flattered. But we started singing together and we could sing in harmony so easily, like it was so natural. For me it just felt like it was meant to be.

I think even from the release of our first album onward we've often felt pigeonholed as a comedy group or a novelty act. And we understand that so much of it is because of what we've presented to people. We've presented to them mugging in photographs, goofy looks, whatever else that we've done over the building of the band's career. And also the fact that people come to a show and they have a great time and they laugh because we are entertainers and at our worst probably addicted to applause and making people laugh is an easy way to keep the show flowing, but at our best we know that we have the ability to make ourselves and the audience feel something, feel something deep and humor is a deep and meaningful feeling.

I think the worst decision we made was on our last album, *Everything to Everyone.* It's an album that's full of angry songs, questioning songs, political songs, very deeply personal songs and we led our first single with a song called "Another Postcard." I think our perspective was, let's lead with this song because it's light; it's fun; it's summertime it's a heavy time. It was 2003 and people were feeling heavy. And we thought there is a lot of heaviness on this record but let's give something to people . . . something fun. Fans thought it was a complete sellout and casual fans heard the song and went that's kind of crappy it's a second rate version of what we've already heard them do and didn't give a really good album the chance it deserved. So we made a mistake by pushing that song first and maybe it shouldn't have even been on the record.

The greatest sacrifice you make as a performer is you compromise your own privacy and your own private time. Not only do you try to balance a road life and a performing life with a home life, which frankly I don't think you can balance. I think something always takes charge and you just have to make sure that the other doesn't disappear. The part that you really do make a sacrifice for is these personal emotions that you have that sometimes we couch in songs about other people but these are thoughts and feelings that we as writers have and we as human beings have. We share those with the world in a way that most people don't. What you risk is other people going "what a horrible person" if some people don't relate to it or if they relate to it they don't want to admit that they do because sometimes there are the dark sides of being a person, the angry, jealous, vindictive person that also appears in songs I write.

ABOUT THE AUTHOR

ABOUT BRUCE WARREN

Bruce Warren was a founding co-producer of *World Cafe*, and is currently the Assistant General Manager of Programming at WXPN-FM in Philadelphia. Bruce started out in the music business as a freelance music journalist. He has been an A&R consultant for Warner Brothers Records and has won numerous music industry awards as Programmer of the Year. When he's not listening to music, he's listening to music. He also manages to spend time with his family, and frequently blogs about music at www.somevelvetblog.blogspot.com, and at www.wxpn.blogspot.com

ABOUT WXPN

WXPN is the award-winning, nationally recognized leader in Triple A radio—a contemporary music format that spans the progressive edges of rock, folk, rhythm and blues, and American roots. Valued for its intelligent presentation of music, knowledgeable hosts, and ability to discover musicians before mainstream radio, WXPN and its nationally distributed *World Cafe*® show have been continually redefining radio for more than two decades.

WXPN is the public radio service of the University of Pennsylvania broadcasting in the Greater Philadelphia/Southern

New Jersey, Worton-Baltimore, Lehigh Valley, and Harrisburg markets, and available worldwide on the Internet at: www.xpn.org and www.XPoNentialMusic.org.

About MusicLab

MusicLab at World Cafe Live is an innovative community-outreach music education program that puts prominent musicians face-to-face with young people, aspiring musicians, and general music lovers. In an interactive format that includes elements of performance, conversation, and Q&A, artists share their experience, demonstrate their technique, and reveal their influences in front of a live audience. Guided by a moderator and by the questions of audience members, artists can punctuate their lesson with musical examples and personal anecdotes. Content at each session is customized to appeal to a specific target audience, so as to provide a meaningful music education experience for all who attend.

ABOUT THE CONTRIBUTORS

(Note: Numbers in parentheses below refer to page numbers.)

Trey Anastasio is the co-founder, guitarist, and songwriter for the seminal jam band Phish. (116, 129)

Jack Barton is the senior director/Triple A for FMQB, *Friday*

Morning Quarterback, a music-industry trade publication. He has been a radio DJ and programmer and has managed artists. (42, 80)

Big & Rich are the superstar country music duo Big Kenny and John Rich. (40)

Joe Bonamassa is a blues and rock guitarist from Utica, New York. At the age of eight he was opening for B.B. King. Bonamassa signed his record deal with Epic at the age of 22, and since 2000 has released six albums. (45)

Billy Bragg is a singer-songwriter from England whose influences include punk and folk music. He recorded two albums of Woody Guthrie songs with Wilco, and his solo recordings on Elektra Records remain high musical watermarks. (82, 140)

Oteil Burbridge is an extraordinary bassist who plays funk, blues, rock, and jazz. He is a founding member of Aquarium Rescue Unit, has performed with The Allman Brothers, and fronts his own band, Oteil & the Peacemakers. (16, 40, 63, 76)

T-Bone Burnett is a guitarist, songwriter, and producer. He produced many significant albums including the Counting Crows' *August And Everything After,* The Wallflowers' *Bringing Down The Horse,* and Elvis Costello's *King of America.* He has produced several film soundtracks, including the Grammy Award-winning soundtrack to *O Brother Where Art Thou.* (142)

Birdie Busch is a singer-songwriter based in Philadelphia. Her debut album *TheWays We Try,* came out in 2006. (114)

Carbon Leaf is a Celtic-influenced rock band from Richmond, Virginia. They grew a nationwide fan base through constant touring and incredible live shows. Their seventh and latest album is *Love, Loss, Hope, Repeat.* (18, 126)

Sean Coakley is founder of Songlines LTD (an independent marketing company), a former executive at major labels, and former manager. See www.songlinesmusic.com. (20, 50, 126)

Bruce Cockburn is a Juno Award-winning singer-songwriter from Canada who has released over 25 albums since his 1970 debut. His classic songs include, "Wondering Where the Lions Are," "If I Had a Rocket Launcher," and "Great Big Love." (79)

Shawn Colvin is a singer-songwriter who rose in popularity in the New York City and Boston folk music scene in the eighties and nineties. In 1998, "Sunny Came Home" won Grammy Awards for Record of the Year and Song of the Year. (143)

Jeff Cook is a former songwriter and the Head of Promotion at

New West Records, and has helped establish the careers of Cake, Widespread Panic, and John Hiatt. (46)

Chick Corea is a highly-influencial jazz pianist who founded the jazz-fusion band, Return To Forever. (63)

Elvis Costello is a singer and songwriter whose work has spanned a highly influential thirty years and has extended to rock and classical music. (135)

Rodney Crowell is a singer-songwriter, guitarist, and producer who's been recognized since the mid-eighties as one of country music's new traditionalists. Crowell produced Rosanne Cash's breakthrough album, *Seven Year Ache.* (144)

Jamie Cullum is a British pianist and singer-songwriter who mixes jazz and pop in a crossover style. (67)

Kathleen Edwards is an alternative country and rock singer-songwriter from Canada. Her 2003 debut album, *Failer,* was hailed by critics as one of the best albums of the year. (17)

James Evans is Head of Promotion at Interscope Records. (136)

Gran Bel Fisher is an Ohio-born singer-songwriter who released his debut album, *Full Moon Cigarette,* in 2006. His songs were featured in television shows including *Grey's Anatomy.* (81, 98)

John Francis is a Philadelphia-based singer-songwriter who has won the ASCAP Sammy Cahn Lyricist Award for the song, "My Love Came to Me Dressed in Red." (25, 54, 64, 68)

Michael Franti formed the politically and socially conscious hip-hop group, the Disposable Heroes Of Hiphoprisy. (89, 144)

Melody Gardot is a blues, folk, jazz, and acoustic-influenced singer-songwriter based in Philadelphia. (29, 83)

Tyler Gibbons is one half of the Philadelphia-based band, Red Heart The Tickler, with Robin MacArthur. (118)

David Gray is a singer-songwriter born in Manchester, England. He released three albums before 1999's *White Ladder,* which included the Top Ten song, "Babylon." (72)

Guster, a band based in Boston, became one of the most successful groups of the nineties through relentless touring and a strong presence on the Internet. Their latest album is *Ganging Up On The Sun* (2006). (44, 116)

Sarah Harmer began her music career in the Canadian band Weeping Tile before going solo in 1999 with her excellent debut album, *You Were Here.* (96)

Warren Haynes is the guitarist, singer and songwriter in Government Mule and he also tours and performs with The Allman Brothers. (16)

Joe Henry is a singer-songwriter and producer. He has produced albums by Ani Difranco, Elvis Costello, Solomon Burke, Aimee Mann, Susan Tedeschi, and others. (133)

Ari Hest is a singer-songwriter from New York City. In 2004, he released *Someone To Tell* to great critical and fan acclaim. (104)

Andy Blackman Hurwitz is the founder of Rope-A-Dope, a label, media, and lifestyle company that produces and releases albums, new media content, and a line of clothing. (127)

Janis Ian is a singer-songwriter who became internationally successful for her Grammy Award-winning "At 17" from her now-classic 1975 album, *Between The Lines.* Her 2006 release is *Folk Is the New Black.* (79, 138, 140)

Mason Jennings is a singer-songwriter and guitarist from Minneapolis. Jennings became the first artist on Modest Mouse frontman Isaac Brock's Epic Records imprint, Glacial Pace, and released *Boneclouds* in 2006. (53, 113)

Keane consists of childhood friends from England—vocalist Tom

Chaplin, drummer Richard Hughes, and keyboardist Tim Rice-Oxley. Their 2004 debut *Hopes And Fears* was an international hit, and was followed up by 2006's *Under The Iron Sea.* (121)

Mark Knopfler is a guitarist, singer and songwriter, and founder of the legendary rock band Dire Straits. (66)

Kufie Knotts is a songwriter, vocalist, rapper, MC and musician based in Philadelphia. He performs with the Dave Quicks Trio. (122)

Sonny Landreth was born in Mississippi and settled in Lafayette, Louisiana. His first professional gig was with zydeco legend Clifton Chenier. His distinct and unique slide and regular guitar playing marks his exhilarating solo albums as well as his work with The Goners, John Hiatt's touring and performing band. (17, 36, 45, 73, 76)

Jennifer Lasker is the President of Lasker Management and represents artists and record producers. (65)

Amos Lee is a Philadelphia-native singer, songwriter, and guitarist. His recent album, *Supply And Demand* was released in 2006 by Blue Note Records. (41)

Helen Leicht is the mid-day host at WXPN-FM in Philadelphia and the director of WXPN's Philly Local music service. Helen has been in broadcasting for 30 years. (71)

Michaela Majoun is the host of the Morning Show at WXPN-FM, 88.5FM in Philadelphia and heard around the world at www.xpn.org. (117)

Aimee Mann led the eighties pop/new-wave band 'Til Tuesday, and had a Top 20 hit song with "Voices Carry" in 1985. She began her solo career in 1993 with *Whatever*. Mann has consistently released excellent albums, including the soundtrack to the critically acclaimed motion picture, *Magnolia*. (66, 96, 148)

Charlotte Martin is an extremely talented, emotive songwriter, singer, and keyboardist. Her decision to leave RCA records after her 2004 release was one of the best of her career. She now runs and owns her own record company, and co-produced her 2006 release *Stromata*. (12, 30, 103)

Dave Matthews started out in the Charlottesville, Virginia music scene and today is one of pop music's most successful touring and recording musicians. The South African vocalist/guitarist and songwriter formed the Dave Matthews Band in the early nineties, and his band continues to tour incessantly. (72, 121)

Michael McDonald got his start singing backup with Steely Dan before becoming a full-fledged member of The Doobie Brothers in 1977. In 1982, McDonald released his first solo album, and continues to see his music perched at the top of both the sales and radio charts. (28, 36, 60)

Brian McTear is a Philadelphia producer and member of the band, Bitter Bitter Weeks. (62, 135, 137)

Johnny Meister is a music programmer and has been the host of *The Blues Show* on WXPN-FM in Philadelphia for 29 years. He received the prestigious "Keepin' The Blues Alive" award from The Blues Foundation in 2000. (70)

Ingrid Michaelson is a singer-songwriter and pianist from New York City. She was one of five co-winners of the 2006 Mountain Stage New Song contest for her song, "Breakable." (38)

Mutlu is a Turkish-American singer-songwriter and guitarist who mines folk, soul, reggae, hip-hop, Brazilian jazz, and acoustic music. (74, 97)

Alexi Murdoch is a singer-songwriter from Scotland. Chosen as one of *Rolling Stone's* Artists to Watch in 2006, his debut release holds the honor of being CD Baby's all-time number-one selling record. His 2006 release is *Time Without Consequence*. (146)

Willie Nelson is a country music legend whose career continues to thrive with *Songbird*, his 2006 release produced by Ryan Adams. As a songwriter and performer since the mid-fifties, Nelson's impact on country, pop music, and pop culture has been deep and wide. (107)

Aaron Neville is a Grammy Award-winning legendary musician from New Orleans who records as a solo artist and is also a member of The Neville Brothers. (150)

Old Crow Medicine Show is a five-piece band of traditional folk and bluegrass revivalists with rock and roll attitude. Their second album, *Big Iron World*, was released in 2006. (133)

John Ondrasik is a singer, songwriter, producer, and keyboardist as well as the creative force, voice and the main member of the hugely popular and platinum award-winning band, Five For Fighting. In 2001, Ondrasik had his first number-one hit song, "Superman (It's Not Easy)." (55, 69)

Steven Page is the lead singer, songwriter and guitarist for the Barenaked Ladies. (153)

David Poe is a singer-songwriter from New York City, and is also the co-founder of The Artists Den, a collaborative live-performance collective of musicians. (77)

Radiohead is one of the UK's most important bands of the last fifteen years. Starting with their 1993 hit song "Creep," Radiohead has continuously pushed musical and creative boundaries on albums like *OK Computer, Kid A, Hail To The Thief,* and *Amnesiac*—each in their own right an indispensable album of the modern era. Lead singer Thom Yorke released his solo debut in 2006 entitled, *The Eraser.* (133)

Bonnie Raitt got her start playing the folk and R&B clubs in Boston in the sixties. Raitt finally achieved immense success with her tenth album, *Nick Of Time,* which released in 1989, went to the top of the U.S. music charts, and won three Grammy Awards. In 1988 she co-founded the Rhythm and Blues Foundation, which works to improve royalties, financial conditions, and recognition for a whole generation of R&B pioneers. The nine-time Grammy Award winner was inducted in to the Rock and Roll Hall of Fame in 2000. (41, 129)

Dan Reed is founder of the "Non-Comm" music conference, an annual gathering of public radio programmers, musicians, and industry people. He is also the Music Director at WXPN-FM and Talent Relations Manager for *World Cafe.* (89)

Nate Reuss is songwriter and singer and guitarist in the band, The Format, a power pop and rock influenced band from Arizona. (130)

Amy Rigby began her career performing in the mid-eighties in the alternative country band The Last Roundup, and then later in the all-girl group The Shams. (82)

Josh Ritter is a singer-songwriter from Moscow, Idaho, who debuted with a self-release album in 1999. Ritter's 2006 album *The Animal Years* was released to great critical acclaim. (134, 141)

Marc A. Roberge is the lead singer and rhythm guitarist of the band O.A.R. (Of A Revolution), which went from being a local college rock band at Ohio State to a stadium headlining act and a Billboard chart-topping success story. (14)

Phil Roy is a native Philadelphia singer-songwriter whose songs have been recorded by Ray Charles, The Neville Brothers, Los Lonely Boys, Joe Cocker, Guster, Pops Staples, Mavis Staples, and Eddie Money. (49, 108)

Emily Saliers is a co-member (with Amy Ray) of the Indigo Girls. (24)

Joe Sample is a jazz keyboardist who was a founding member of the Jazz Crusaders. They dropped the "jazz" from their name in the seventies and transitioned from traditional jazz to electronic and fusion. (28, 73, 90, 97)

Scot Sax is a multi-instrumentalist whose first band, Wanderlust, went from jamming in a basement to landing a record deal with RCA, touring with Collective Soul and opening for the WHO—all within 2 years. (37, 91)

Brian Seymour has long been a favorite on the local Philadelphia music scene as an independent singer-songwriter in full command of his career from both the creative and business side of the profession. (26, 100, 121)

John Schoenberger is the Triple A and Americana Editor for *Radio & Records*, a music industry trade publication. (129)

Mindy Smith was born on Long Island, New York. In 1998 she moved to Nashville to pursue a career in music. Her big break came when she was asked to contribute to *Just Because I'm A Woman: The Songs Of Dolly Parton*, a prestigious tribute to the country superstar. (53, 102)

Candi Staton began her career as a Gospel singer before recording numerous R&B hits in the sixties and seventies. In the mid-seventies, Staton returned to the charts with several disco hits, and since then has released secular and Gospel albums, including the recent *His Hands*. (151)

Stephen Stills is a singer, songwriter, guitarist, and producer known for his contributions to two of rock music's most legendary and enduring bands, Buffalo Springfield and Crosby, Stills, Nash & Young. (144)

Sting began his career with Andy Summers and Stewart Copeland in The Police, who, by the early eighties, were the most popular rock band in the world based on the strength of hits like "Roxanne," "Message In A Bottle," and "Every Little Thing She Does Is Magic." At the height of their popularity, The Police broke up. Since then, Sting continues to endure as one of pop music's most important musicians. (96, 106)

Richard Thompson's career began as a co-founding member of the influential sixties British folk and rock band, Fairport Convention. A guitarist, songwriter, and singer, Thompson has had a long and prosperous career as a solo artist. (113)

They Might Be Giants are singer-songwriters John Linnell and John Flansburgh. (44)

Vivek Tiwary is the founder/CEO of The Tiwary Entertainment Group and StarPolish.com. He is involved in production, management, marketing, and investment in theater, music, television, and film. Prior to founding TEG and StarPolish, he held a number of major-label music-industry positions. He has worked with artists covering the entire musical spectrum, from Bon

Jovi and Allen Ginsberg to Pearl Jam and Shania Twain. Tiwary is also the Co-Founder of Musicians On Call, a nonprofit organization that uses music and entertainment to complement the healing process. (51, 59)

Allen Toussaint is a music legend from New Orleans who has had a lifetime of the highest achievement as a songwriter, producer, arranger, session player, and pianist, and who has written classics like "Sneaking Sally Through The Alley," "Working In A Coalmine," and "Yes We Can." (67)

KT Tunstall rose to fame with the release of her 2006 American debut, *Eye to the Telescope*. The Scottish singer-songwriter and guitarist's hit song is, "Black Horse & the Cherry Tree." (97, 107, 116)

Laura Veirs is a singer, songwriter, and guitarist from Seattle whose recent album, *Year Of Meteors*, was released in 2005 on Nonesuch Records. (145)

Neil Young came to America from his hometown of Toronto in the mid-sixties where he joined Buffalo Springfield and then Crosby, Stills, Nash & Young. In a 40-year career, he has had a profound effect on pop culture, songwriting, performing, and the music industry as a whole. Like Bob Dylan, Young is a songwriter and artist of such incredible depth and significance, few words can do justice to his incredible body of work. (90)

Warren Zevon was a musician and songwriter who sadly passed away in 2003. He was noted for his offbeat, sardonic view of life which was reflected in his dark, sometimes humorous songs, which often incorporated political and historical themes. In the mid-seventies Zevon became associated with the West Coast singer-songwriter scene which included artists like Jackson Browne, The Eagles and Linda Ronstadt; Jackson Browne also produced his now classic self-titled 1976 release. While Zevon is best known for a string of hit songs throughout his career including "Werewolves Of London," "Excitable Boy," and "Lawyers, Guns And Money," he's also responsible for writing some tender, beautiful tunes like "Carmelita," and "Keep Me In Your Heart." (37, 106)

RESOURCES

WEB SITES

BBC One Music—www.bbc.co.uk/radio1/onemusic/
The BBC's One Music Web site is designed for anyone interested in becoming a professional musician. There is in-depth help

and advice on making music, finding jobs in the industry, and how-to counsel on just about every facet of music.

Future Of Music Coalition—www.futureofmusic.org
The Future of Music Coalition is a not-for-profit collaboration between members of the music, technology, public policy, and intellectual property law communities.

Just Plain Folks—www.jpfolks.com
Just Plain Folks is an online networking community of songwriters, recording artists, music publishers, record labels, performing arts societies, educational institutions, recording studios and engineers, producers, legal professionals, publicists and journalists, publications, music manufacturers, and retailers.

Lyricist.com—www.lyricist.com
Jeff Mallett's songwriter site is an excellent collection of links to interviews with songwriters on songwriting, songwriter Web sites, legal and business sites, magazines, books, and organizations that lend support to songwriters, publishing, and copyright companies.

Music Business Academy—www.musicbizacademy.com
Music Business Academy is a Web site for independent musicians in the business of selling, promoting or doing music on the Internet.

Performing Songwriter—www.performingsongwriter.com

This Web site is the companion to the outstanding magazine, *Performing Songwriter*. There are interviews with musicians as well as a robust collection of resources including articles about the business of music, guest columns from musicians about making music, and interviews with emerging and established musicians on subjects from technology to songwriting.

RAIN (Radio and Internet Newsletter)—www.kurthanson.com

Created and edited by Kurt Hanson, this is a one-stop source for key issues about radio, the music industry, and the Internet.

StarPolish—www.StarPolish.com

StarPolish is a collaborative effort between artists and music industry professionals who are dedicated to educating and empowering artists, with an emphasis on artist advocacy and artist development. The Web site features many interviews with artists about the music business and making music, as well as articles about the art and business of music production, booking shows, promotion and marketing, music publishing and rights, music and the Internet, and management and legal issues.

SUGGESTED READING

All You Need to Know about the Music Business,
    by Donald S. Passman.

The Business of Artist Management, by Xavier M. Frascona, Jr.
    and H. Lee Hetherington.

*This Business of Music: The Definitive Guide to the Music
    Industry, Ninth Edition,* by M. William Krasilovsky.

*The Future of Music: Manifesto for the Digital Music
    Revolution,* by David Kusek and Gerd Leonhard.

This Business of Music Marketing and Promotion,
    by Ted Lathrop.

Legal Aspects of the Music Industry: An Insider's View,
    by Richard Schulenberg.

*Making and Marketing Music: The Musician's Guide to
    Financing, Distributing and Promoting Albums,*
    by Jodi Summers.

*What They'll Never Tell You about the Music Business: The
    Myths, Secrets, Lies (& a Few Truths),* by Peter M. Thall.

How to Make It in the New Music Business: Lessons, Tips and Inspiration from Music's Biggest and Best, by Robert Wolff.